Fantastic Wedding Finales

About the Series

The Romantic Wedding Rituals series is a collection of definitive guides to symbolic rituals used in wedding and commitment ceremonies.

Other titles in the series

Unity Candle and Sand Ceremony
A Definitive Guide to the Creative Use of Candles and Sand Rituals in Wedding and Commitment Ceremonies

How to Write Vows that Wow!

The Gay Groom's Guide to Writing Your Vows

The Lesbian Bride's Guide to Writing Your Vows

55 Loving Ways to Remember
A Definitive Guide to Including Those Who Have Passed in Your Wedding Ceremony and Celebration

Perfect Wedding Processionals
A Definitive Guide to Making a Grand Entrance for your Wedding or Commitment Ceremony

Forthcoming Titles

The Rose Ceremony and Flower Rituals
A Definitive Guide to the Creative Use of Flowers in Wedding and Commitment Ceremonies

Other planned titles will cover the use of Pebbles and Stones, Handfasting and the use of Ribbons and Cords, and Wine Rituals.

Disclaimer

Although Jennifer Cram has taken every care in preparing and writing this book, she accepts no liability for any errors, omissions, misuse, or misunderstandings on the part of any person who uses it or the associated website. Reliance on the information and material in this book and the associated website, including linked or recommended resources, shall be at your sole risk. The author specifically disclaims any implied warranties of fitness for any particular purpose and accepts no responsibility for any damage, injury, or loss occasioned to any person as a result of relying on any material included, omitted, or implied.

Fantastic Wedding Finales

A Definitive Guide to Recessionals,
Tosses, Releases, Jumping the Broom,
and Other Creative Grand Finales
for your Wedding or Commitment Ceremony

Jennifer Cram
Authorized Marriage Celebrant

Romantic Wedding Rituals Series

Fantastic Wedding Finales
A Definitive Guide to Recessionals, Tosses, Releases, Jumping the Broom,
and Other Creative Grand Finales for your Wedding
or Commitment Ceremony

First edition.
©Jennifer Cram 2014. All rights reserved.

Front Cover photograph   © Maksim Pasko | Dreamstime.com
Cover Background photograph   © Jinaiji | Dreamstime.com

ISBN-10: 1461165229
ISBN-13: 978-1461165224

SERIES FOREWORD

Wedding and commitment ceremonies require beautiful words. It is the words of the ceremony, particularly those of the promises that the couple makes, that create their union and emphasize what is important to them. However, it is the visual images that linger in the minds of the guests, provide opportunities for amazing photographs, and create truly memorable moments. What would a wedding ceremony be without the image of the ring being slipped onto the bride's finger? Who at a wedding or commitment ceremony doesn't eagerly anticipate the highpoint of the ceremony – the kiss? These images evoke the tender emotions that make ceremonies special.

Great wedding ceremony images add drama to the ceremony. Rituals provide the opportunity tell a story that enriches the sentiments that have been expressed and enhances the promises that have been exchanged. Rituals also provide opportunities to express the warmth of the relationship between the couple, their families and friends, and to demonstrate generosity of spirit in acknowledging that every relationship needs the support of others. It is this combination of imagination and creativity with warmth and generosity of spirit that creates a magical ceremony. Inviting those attending your marriage or commitment ceremony to participate in the ritual in some way provides an opportunity to transform the ceremony from being a performance witnessed by an audience of family and friends to a community experience. Including a ritual is also a very effective way to bridge a language gap where you have guests who are not native speakers of the primary language in which the ceremony is conducted.

Rituals in weddings have become fashionable. What a celebrity does in her wedding becomes the *must-have* for countless brides, encouraged by wedding planners who provide a 'check the box' list. Moreover, couples come to believe that there is an 'authorized' form of the ritual to which they are required to adhere. Nothing could be further from the truth.

A ritual is a symbolic act, a visual expression of an intention. When used in a ritual, a symbol is a means by which we convey, in an intuitive rather than logical way, the transcendent. Therefore, a genuine symbol does what it symbolizes. The exchange of vows and rings, now an integral part of any marriage or commitment ceremony, both symbolize and create the union.

Mindless replication or repetition of any ritual has the potential to strip the words, the performance, and the underlying idea of meaning, and therefore should be avoided. For maximum impact, any symbolic ritual you include in your ceremony needs to truly reflect your unique and wonderful relationship with each other, and/or with your family members and friends. It needs to be personal. It needs to be something you have made your own otherwise it becomes a meaningless distraction.

Reading about a ritual is not enough. Try it out before you make the final decision to include it in your ceremony. Does it feel comfortable for you? Will those attending your wedding 'get it' or will it make them feel uncomfortable or confused? Or even worse, will the ritual seem totally alien to them or just plain silly?

This is not to say you should never include a ritual that no one in your community has ever seen before, but you should assess the extent to which there is a genuine connection between the ritual, the sentiments expressed elsewhere in your ceremony, and your heritage.

This last is particularly important. Avoid cultural appropriation, taking something from a culture with which you have no connection. Particularly, be a little skeptical about claims made that the ritual has its origins 'long ago and far away'. In many cases invented rituals are given an unnecessary and equally invented history to confer legitimacy, when no such history is needed.

When you have chosen to include a particular ritual in your ceremony, think carefully about what it means for you, how you can make it your own. And rehearse and rehearse. For best effect the ritual should be effortlessly performed.

Ensure that both your photographer and your videographer are fully briefed before the day so they know what to expect and where to position themselves to capture the best visual record of the ritual. You may find it useful to provide them with a written summary of how the ritual will unfold.

On the day take your time. Do not rush through the ritual. You will be rewarded with a special moment and a wonderful photographic record.

Enjoy!

CONTENTS

INTRODUCTION

C losing rituals are both visually appealing and emotionally exciting finales that highlight the end of the marriage or commitment ceremony after the pronouncement and kiss. They may immediately precede the recessional, constitute part of the recessional, or be carried out immediately after it. Some closing rituals – such as the jumping of the broom, the breaking of the glass, the recessional, and arches of honor – are also transition rituals, that is rituals that are not part of a wedding or commitment ceremony but rather take place after the service is concluded. Transition rituals symbolize the passage of the couple into married life. Other closing rituals allow the guests to participate in an exuberant expression of good wishes and blessings for the couple.

Although a wedding or commitment ceremony is a joyous occasion, it can also be a tense experiences for everyone present, not just for the couple. The words of the ceremony relate not only to the couple, but also serve as a commentary relevant to the lives of the guests, and this stirs up emotions so that tension builds throughout the ceremony. An effective finale releases the tension and allows a spirit of gaiety and celebration to take over.

The most familiar ritual, the recessional, has for generations been punctuated by the throwing of grain, or substitutes, over the couple as a blessing or fertility rite. Over the years what is tossed and where and when it is tossed has changed as wedding ceremonies and customs have evolved and the range and type of venue where the ceremony is held has expanded. Restrictions brought about by legislative and policy changes have also created the need for creative change.

But rather than newer tosses superseding older ones, what has happened has been a broadening of options. Confetti and rice, though out of favor, are still thrown as are the more frequently seen choices of flower petals and bubbles.

The practice continues to evolve, with releases of balloons, butterflies and doves becoming more common. However, though the most common finale, tosses and releases are by no means the only form of finale suitable for a wedding ceremony.

Most finales can also be used for your exit from your reception, however, extra opportunities for interaction with your guests are available, enabling you to say farewell and thanks in a very personal way.

This book will guide you through a wide range of ways to end your wedding on a high note. It also provides you with information about practical requirements and the .historic and symbolic background to familiar and less-familiar rituals.

Enjoy your journey through the options and ideas, and have a great wedding with a fantastically exciting and photogenic finale!

PART ONE:
THE RECESSIONAL

WHAT IS THE RECESSIONAL?

The joyous climax to one of life's most memorable occasions, the recessional is an age-old transition ritual where the couple moves forward into their married life. At the conclusion of the ceremony, the newly married couple, followed by the bridal party and their parents, makes their way back up the aisle. It is a triumphant moment and the guests often burst into spontaneous applause to signal their joy that you are now married.

You can make your recessional into something extra special in a number of very easy to implement ways:

- By your choice of music
- By pausing for an additional 'spontaneous' kiss halfway down the aisle
- By adding other finale rituals such as a toss or a guard of honor, or
- By emulating a royal/presidential walkabout – pausing to shake hands and share a few words with guests (or accept congratulatory hugs and kisses) as you slowly make your way down the aisle.

STRUCTURING THE RECESSIONAL

While a recessional is an important part of most weddings how it is structured may differ depending on local customs or cultural practices. While the bride and groom always lead the recessional[1], who is on the right and who on the left, and who follows and in what order, is not universal. However, should you wish to diverge from local custom, there is no reason why you shouldn't. The structure of the recessional is custom and tradition, not law.

Who walks where?

The bride and groom lead the recessional, followed by the bridal party. Usually, the best man and chief bridesmaid walk immediately behind the bride and groom, followed, in order of seniority, by the rest of the party, with the parents bringing up the rear. This allows the parents to be the first to congratulate the happy couple.

A common and very practical variation is for the flower girl(s) to follow immediately after the bride and groom.

---

[1] An exception is a Scottish wedding, where a piper always leads both the processional and the recessional

Having the bride's father escort the groom's mother, and the groom's father escort the bride's mother, is an effective low-key way of acknowledging that the marriage has created a new, extended family.

How to hold hands?

There are basically three ways to walk back down the aisle

- For an informal look and feel just hold hands
- For a more formal look the groom offers his arm and the bride puts her hand in the crook of his elbow.
- For the most formal look the groom holds his forearm parallel to the floor and the bride places her hand on the top of his hand. A more intimate variation is for the bride to curl her fingers into the groom's palm.

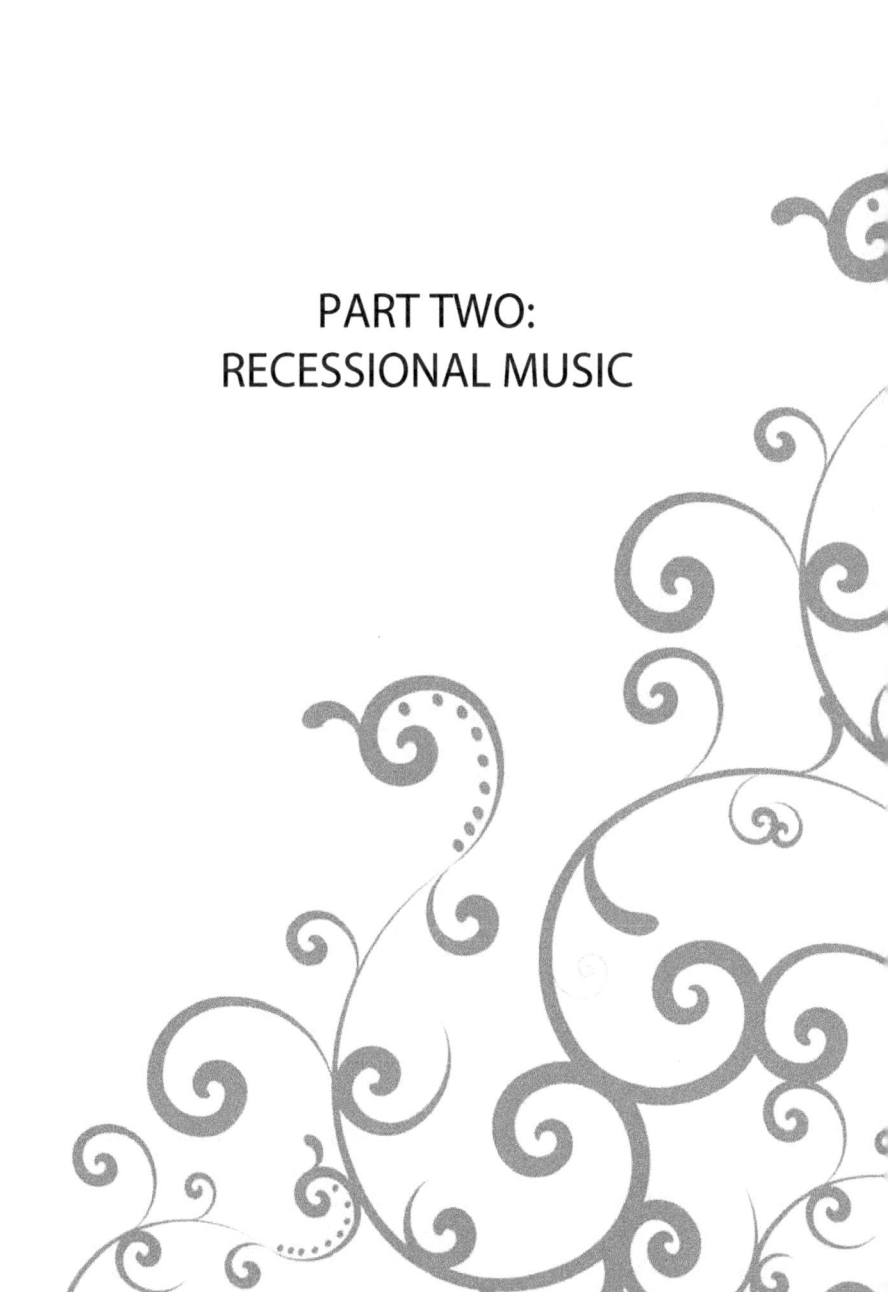

PART TWO:
RECESSIONAL MUSIC

CHOOSING MUSIC FOR YOUR RECESSIONAL

The music you choose for your exit at the end of the ceremony is the climax of the ceremony so should be up-beat, celebratory and happy, conveying the euphoria of the moment. Music ramps up the emotion, and while the music for the processional (entrance) conveys a sense of expectation, the music for the processional conveys the fulfillment of that expectation. Therefore, while it is a personal choice, your choice should communicate your just-married joy to everyone present.

While most couples choose processional music that is traditional, elegant and more low-key, choosing music for the recessional has different purpose and therefore requires a different frame of mind and therefore opens up a world of possibilities.

Many couples avoid classical music because they feel unsure of their capacity to choose 'correctly', or they make a default choice - the traditional Mendelssohn *Wedding March* the traditional Mendelssohn *Wedding March* from *A Midsummer Night's Dream*. One of the most widely recognized pieces of music in the western world, it was first used at a wedding in 1847.[2]. However, it became popular

---

[2] At the wedding of Tom Daniel and Dorothy Carew in St Peter's Church, Tiverton, Devon, England.

only after Queen Victoria's daughter selected it for her wedding to Prince Frederick William of Prussia in 1858.

There is nothing wrong with choosing it, in fact, if you want to give the nod to tradition in an otherwise modern and personal ceremony, it is a great choice because everyone will recognize it, it is a wonderful piece of music for creating the right atmosphere, and it is easy to walk to at a brisk pace.

Another popular choice is *Toccata,* the final movement of the French composer Widor's *Symphony for Organ No. 5*, composed in 1879.

Nonetheless, the first principle to adhere to is that your choice of music should be a conscious one, taking into account both the possibilities and the constraints applicable to your wedding.

While the processional is simply the signal that the ceremony is about to start, the recessional is more than merely a signal that the ceremony has ended. It serves that purpose but it also creates a transition between the solemnity and reverence of the ceremony and the party mood of what follows. The celebration is about to get underway and it is appropriate to signal this in your choice of music.

I've had couples exit to a themes from a video games, a medley of traditional wedding staples combined with the anthems of the teams they support, and every type of popular song you imaginable. Choosing music that is not commonly used for wedding recessionals is a simple way of ensuring that your recessional is exciting, distinctive and a reflection of you.

You should decide whether you will have live or recorded music very early in the process.. Live music is something truly special at a wedding; however, recorded music can give you a wider choice, including big orchestra/big band sound, at a much lower cost.

Making the old classical staples new

Choosing one of the old familiar classical pieces has the advantage that your guests will 'get it' and you can make even the most familiar piece fresh and interesting by giving it a little twist. Your guests will be delighted when you walk back up the aisle to something that is both familiar and unique.

- The Mendelssohn *Wedding March* is frequently played on an organ or a recorded orchestral version is used. It is also lovely when played on a wide variety of solo instruments from violin to flute, played in an unexpected style, for example jazz, blue grass, or swing, or by a brass trio or quartet.

- Ask your organist to change the registrations, or your musicians to tweak the tempo or to be creative in their interpretation of the piece.

Traditional wedding songs

Another safe choice is one of the wedding or love songs that have been around long enough to be accepted as 'traditional'. These include *All You Need is Love* (The Beatles). Use the original, another artist's version, a live singer, or an instrumental version.

Modern recessional music

Many modern brides make a very personal choice from a contemporary playlist. If you go down this route it is important to

- Listen carefully to the lyrics to make sure they are suitable for a wedding. It is hard at times to differentiate between a love song and a break-up song.

- If the song has personal meaning in your relationship include a note in your wedding program to explain the significance of your choice.

Giving contemporary music a classical feel

Hire a string quartet or other classical musician(s) to play a classical interpretation of a pop song that is special to you. If you have good musicians, they will be able to develop a version of any song you like.

Affirm your cultural heritage

Affirming your cultural values choosing music for your recessional that acknowledges your heritage not only adds a very personal touch, it speaks volumes about your values.

Don't forget that a medley can surprise and delight ...

If you wish to create a medley for your recessional, readily available modern technology means you are not restricted to using live musicians. Nor are you limited to an either/or choice between styles of music. I've had several couples meld the Mendelssohn *Wedding March* with themes from Star Wars, Broadway musicals, Beatles staples, and other wonderful classical pieces such as Beethoven's *Ode to Joy* (a particular favorite of mine because you cannot fail to be uplifted by it).

You can borrow from the theatre and use a medley to reprise music played for the processional and during the ceremony, interspersed with an identifiable recessional choice such as the Mendelssohn *Wedding March*.

In addition, you can use music to express values you hold dear. For example, a recessional medley comprising the Mendelssohn *Wedding March* interwoven with a sung or an instrumental rendering of the melody sections of *Same Love* (Macklemore and Lewis).

... Or that a choir is an option

Your recessional does not have to be restricted to instrumental music. Choosing a choir or choral group widens your possible choices. For example, you can exit to a hymn or to a popular song with meaningful lyrics.

Fast forward to the melody

Whether you include a popular song in a medley or use as a stand-alone choice, for maximum impact cut the introductory bars and start at the beginning of the melody.

Before you choose your music you need to know ...

- If the policies of your ceremony venue puts limitations on your choice of music or how it is played. Some denominations ban secular music. In many churches this includes the Mendelssohn *Wedding March* together with modern secular songs. Interestingly enough, in England and Wales, where a Registrar will attend a licensed venue to conduct a civil marriage ceremony, many Registrars also ban this piece together with the *Here Comes the Bride* (the Wagner *Bridal Chorus* from *Lohengrin*) citing as the reason that, though secular, these pieces are associated with church weddings.

- What is the policy of your church or venue in relation to hiring outside musicians. Some churches only allow use of the in-house organist, and some venues may have in-house musicians or preferred suppliers.

- Which, if any, instrument is available. For example, is there an organ or piano on site.

- What, if any, equipment is available to play recorded music.

- What styles of music will best express your personalities and suit your ceremony.

- How long it will take for the whole wedding party to exit.

And you need to reach agreement on the following ...

- Do you want to make a statement with a modern piece or would you prefer to stick to one of the traditional favourites?

- Are you going to use a single piece of music or a medley?

- Does the music you're considering reflect your personalities as a couple?
- Will your music choice be familiar to your guests, or if not familiar, will they recognize that it is celebratory?
- Will anyone important to you be offended by your choice?
- Are you going to use the same music for the entire process (recessional plus exit of guests) or change the mood for the exit of the guests

You will need to consult with live musicians as to

- Whether the music you have chosen will translate well to the instrument(s) they play. Pieces originally scored for a solo keyboard instrument or pieces originally scored for a larger ensemble may not translate satisfactorily.
- Whether the musical line of the lyrics of a song is compatible with an instrumental version of the song.

Be prepared to spend some time researching and selecting live musicians. Ask for a repertoire list so you know what they already have and look for a match if possible. Most musicians will charge extra if they have to learn a new piece or are required to make a special arrangement of a piece.

TIMING YOUR RECESSIONAL MUSIC

H ow much time your recessional will take depends on the length of the aisle and the number of people who will be participating.

While the length of the processional music *is* critical because you need to ensure that the music doesn't run out before everyone is in place at the altar, nor do you want the bridal party standing in place while the music plays on and on and on, the same does not apply for the recessional music. A bridal party has made their exit. It is preferable that the music continues until the guests have also exited, however that can be achieved by repeating the piece or by segucing to a different piece.

Before you finalize your musical choice you need to know how long the aisle is, i.e. how long it will take for someone to walk the length of the aisle at a good brisk pace. Typically, the bridal party walks faster when exiting than when entering. They will also walk closer together, so allow for three paces between, and more people will participate as the parents usually bring up the rear of the recessional in order to ensure that they are the first to congratulate the couple.

The only way to calculate how much music you need is to pace it out, time how long it takes for one person to make the full walk and multiply by the number of individuals/pairs in the processional, and allow for the extra time taken up by the spacing.

Example:

The aisle is 50 paces long and there are the couple, three pairs of bridesmaids/groomsmen/flower girls plus two sets of parents. Total is therefore 300 paces. To that you need to add 5 "spaces" of 3 paces each to the total of 300 paces that, collectively, you, will walk.

When you allow for the spacing, the exit of the group will take approximately as long as it would take one individual to walk 315 paces. To accommodate that will need a piece of music that is a minimum of 6.5 times[3] as long as the time one individual needs to walk back up the aisle[4].

It is highly unlikely that you will be able to match the length of your chosen piece to exactly the amount of time your processional will take. Therefore, you should also decide how you are going to ensure that the music is neither too short nor too long. Some options are:

- Choose a piece of music that can be faded out or tapered off once the church or ceremony space is nearly empty. For recorded music fade the music out slowly. Live musicians will need to play to the end of the measure
- Repeat the main melody as many times as necessary, reserving the final section to be played only once at the end.

---

[3] Actually 6.3 times but it is best to allow a little extra
[4] To ascertain the timing, have each couple walk back up the aisle. Ensure that the females will be wearing the shoes they will be wearing at the wedding. People walk differently in heels and each will walk at a slightly different pace because the length of their stride will differ. Work on an average!

MUSIC SUGGESTIONS FOR YOUR RECESSIONAL

Your recessional music is the celebratory climax to your ceremony – and the music that creates the transition to party mode. For best results choose your music carefully and ensure it is played at an appropriate volume.

This list includes many old favorites and some less well-known selections. Consider it a starting point in your search for the perfect music for your fantastic recessional.

Classical

Bach: Allegro from Brandenburg Concerto No. 1
Bach: Allegro from Brandenburg Concerto no. 4 in G
Bach: Allegro from Organ Concerto in G Major)
Bach: Arioso from Cantata No. 156
Bach: Badinerie from Orchestral Suite No. 2 in B minor
Bach: Prelude in C Major
Beethoven: Andante Con Molto from Symphony no. 5
Beethoven: Ode to Joy from Symphony no. 9
Boellman: Allegro (Menuet Gothique) from Suite Gothique opus 25
Clarke: Trumpet Tune in D Major (Prince of Denmark's March) *(often incorrectly attributed to Henry Purcell)*
Dubois: Toccata in G Major

Geminiani: Presto from Concerto Grosso in D Minor, opus 2, no. 3

Grieg: Praeludium from Holberg Suite opus. 40

Grieg: Triumphal March

Handel :The Arrival of the Queen of Sheba from Solomon

Handel: Air from Water Music Suite

Handel: Allegro Maestoso from Water Music Suite

Handel: Finale from Water Music Suite

Handel: Hallelujah Chorus from the Messiah

Handel: Hornpipe from Water Music Suite

Handel: La Rejouissance from Music for the Royal Fireworks

Handel: Largo from Xerxes

Lang: Tuba Tune in D Major opus 15

Lemmens: Fanfare in D Major from École d'Orgue,

Mendelssohn – Allegro in C minor from Organ Sonata No. 2

Mendelssohn: Wedding March from A Midsummer Night's Dream,

Mouret – Rondeau from *Suite de symphonies*

Purcell: Rondeau (from Abdelezar)

Strauss:Radetzky March opus 228

Tartini: Sonata in G Major opus 1

Vierne : Finale from Symphony No. 1 for Organ opus 14

Walton: Crown Imperial Coronation March

Widor: Toccata from Symphonie 5, opus 42

Classical religious, including choral works

Bach: In Thee is Gladness

Bach: Jesu, joy of man's desiring

Bach: May God smile on you

Bach: Now thank we all our God (Nun danket)

Bach: Sheep May Safely Graze

Batten: O sing joyfully

Beethoven: Ode to Joy (the hymn *Joyful Joyful we adore Thee*)

Benedetto: Psalm 19 (*The Heavens Declare the Glory of God*)

Carter: Go before us, O Lord

Handel: Rejoice greatly, O daughter of Zion from the Messiah
Handel – Hallelujah Chorus from The Messiah
Manz: God of Grace and God of Glory
Mathias: Let the people praise thee, O God
Mozart: Laudate Dominum (Psalm 117)

Movie/TV show themes

A Whole New World (theme from *Aladdin*)
Gonna Fly Now (theme from *Rocky*)
I'll be there for you (the theme from *Friends*)
Man in Motion (theme from *St Elmo's Fire*)
Rondeau (theme from *Masterpiece*)
Rondeau (intro song for video game *Thunder Castle*)
Soul Bossa Nova (theme from *Austin Powers*)
Storybook Love (*Princess Bride* Theme)
The Imperial March (Theme from *Star Wars*)
The Liberty Bell (theme from *Monty Python*)
The Newly-wed Game theme
The Raiders' March (theme from *Indiana Jones*)
Thus spake Zarathustra (theme from *2001 A Space Odyssey*

Modern recessional Songs/music

A Moment Like This - Kelly Clarkson
A Wedding Thank You - Mikki Viereck
All My Life - K Ci & Jojo
Ain't That Love – Ray Charles
All I Want is You – Barry Louis Polisar
All My Love - Led Zeppelin
All The Way - Celine Dion and Frank Sinatra
All You Need Is Love - The Beatles
Anyone Else But You - The Moldy Peaches
Beautiful Day - U2
Because You Loved Me - Celine Dion
Believe - Lenny Kravitz
Better Life – Keith Urban

Better Together- Jack Johnson's
Breathless – The Corrs
Brighter Than the Sun - Colbie Caillat
Can't Fight this Feeling - REO Speedwagon
Can't Get Enough of Your Love Babe - Barry White
Can't Stop Loving You - Phil Collins
Can't Take My Eyes Off You - Frankie Valli
Celebration – Kool and the Gang
Clocks - Vitamin String Quartet
Crazy In Love – Beyoncé
Crazy Little Thing Called Love – Michael Bublé
Dance Tonight – Paul McCartney
Do You Realize – Flaming Lips
Dog Days are Over – Florence and The Machine
Don't Stop Believing - Vitamin String Quartet
Enter Sandman – Metallica
Everlasting Love – Love Affair
Every time We Touch – Cascada
Final Countdown – Europe
Finally – Ce Ce Penniston
First Day of My Life - Bright Eyes
Flower In The Window – Travis
Fly Me To The Moon – Frank Sinatra
Forever – Mariah Carey
Forever Young – Bob Dylan or Neil Young
Fresh Feeling – Eels
From This Moment On - Cole Porter
Get Ready For This – 2 Unlimited
Get This Party Started – Pink
God Only Knows – Beach Boys
Grow Old With Me - The Postal Service
Happily Ever After - Blu Cantrell
Happy Together – The Turtles
Hello Sunshine - Super Furry Animals
Here and Now – Luther Vandross

Here Comes The Sun – Beatles
Hero – Mariah Carey
Hold My Hand – Hootie and the Blowfish
Home – Edward Sharpe and the Magnetic Zeros
How Sweet It Is – James Taylor or Marvin Gaye
I Do – 98 Degrees
I Found A Reason – Cat Power
I Got You Babe – Sonny & Cher
I Melt With You – Modern Romance
I Wanna Know All Of You – Hardy
I Was Made for You - She & Him
I'm A Believer –The Monkees
I'm Into Something Good - The Bird and The Bee
I'm Yours - Vitamin String Quartet
In My Life – Beatles
It Had To Be You – Harry Connick Jr
It's You It's Me - Kaskade
Joy – Apollo 100
Just Like Heaven – Cure
Keeper Of The Stars – Tracy Byrd
Let My love Open The Door – Pete Townsend
Let's Get Loud – J Lo
Life - Love & Laughter - Donavon Frankenreiter
Like A Star – Corrine Bailey Rae
Linus and Lucy Peanuts Theme - Vince Guaraldi
Living on A Prayer – Bon Jovi
Looks Like We Made It - Barry Manilow
Love - Matt White
L-O-V-E – Michael Buble
L-O-V-E - Nat King Cole
Love Is A Beautiful Thing – Phil Vasser
Love Me Do - The Beatles
Love Story – Taylor Swift
Love To – Mika
Love Train – O'Jays

Love You Madly - Cake
Love Your Ways – Salmonella Dub
Lovely Day – Bill Withers
Marry You - Bruno Mars
My Best Friend – Tim McGraw
Never Gonna Give You Up – Rick Astley
No One - Alicia Keys
Nothing's Going to Stop Us Now – Starship
Paradise By The Dashboard Lights – Meatloaf
Party Like A Rockstar – Shop Boyz
Promise – Ciara
Realize - Colbie Caillat
Rhythm of Love - Plain White T's
Sail Away – David Grey
Show Me Love – Robin
Signed - Sealed - Delivered - Stevie Wonder
Signed, Sealed Delivered, I'm Yours – Stevie Wonder
So Amazing – Beyoncé and Stevie Wonder
Some Kind Of Wonderful – Huey Lewis
Stay Down – Luther Vandross
Stolen – Dashboard Confessional
Stuck On You – Lionel Ritchie
Sunshine of My Life - Stevie Wonder
Sweet Escape – Gwen Stefani
Tenderness – General Public
Thank You For Loving Me – Bon Jovi
The Long and Winding Road - The Beatles
This I swear – Nick Lachey
This Will Be An Everlasting Love – Natalie Cole
This Will Be Our Year - The Zombies
Thunder Road – Bruce Springsteen
Thunderstruck – ACDC
To Be Surprised - Sondre Lerche
Too Late To Turn Back Now – Eddy Cornelius
Truly Madly Deeply – Cascada

Two of Us - Aimee Mann
Until The End Of Time –Justin Timberlake and Beyoncé
Walking on Sunshine – Katrina and the Waves
Way You Move – Outkast
We Are Family – Dream Girls
We Go Together – from the *Grease* Soundtrack
We've Only Just Begun - Carpenters
Wedding Day – Bee Gees
What a Wonderful World – Louis Armstrong
When I'm Sixty-Four - The Beatles
When You Say Nothing At All - Ronan Keating
Wonderful Tonight – Eric Clapton
Wouldn't it be nice – Beach Boys
You Always Make me Smile – Kyle Andrews
You and Me – The Wannadies
You are the Best Thing – Ray La Montagne
You Are The Sunshine Of My Life – Stevie Wonder
You Belong To Me – Jason Wade
You Decorated My Life – Kenny Rogers
You Make My Dreams – Hall and Oats
You to Me Are Everything - Barry White
You're My Best Friend – Queen
You're the World to Me - David Gray
Your Precious Love – Marvin Gaye and Tammi Terrell

JENNIFER CRAM

PART THREE: ARCHES OF HONOR

MILITARY ARCH OF HONOR

Passing through a military arch of swords or sabers (which depends on the branch of the military) is a transition ritual that is meant to ensure the couple' safe passage into married life.

Historically the groom, but now either the bride or groom, must be a serving officer or non-commissioned officer. Each branch of the military has its own protocol. In addition and there may be variations between countries, however, there is a high degree of commonality, including that regardless of nationality or service branch, protocol must be followed to the letter.

- Traditionally the arch is formed outside the church or chapel because unsheathed weapons are never carried in a house of worship. Some houses of worship will allow the arch to be formed in the foyer, so enquire early.
- The arch is usually formed by six or eight military personnel..
- Dress uniform is worn
- The most senior officer takes the left hand front position.
- If more than one branch of the military is involved, as may happen in a cross-service wedding, the most senior officer is in command.

- When the swords or sabers are raised they are rotated clockwise so that the cutting edge will be on top.

- The two sword or saber bearers at the front lower their weapons to block the passage of the couple and demand that they kiss before being allowed to pass. This makes a wonderful photograph.

- Yet another tradition is a gentle "swat to the backside" that the bride receives from the last swordsman. No modern bride should be unpleasantly surprised by this, so make sure that you communicate your wishes very clearly to all concerned if you do not want this tradition followed.

SPORTING OR INTEREST ARCH OF HONOR

You do not have to be a serving member of the military to enjoy the pomp of an arch of honor. You can celebrate your sport or a special interest by walking out under an arch formed by team members or members of your club or interest group, who hold something emblematic of the sport or interest over your heads to create the tunnel through which you will walk. For example:

- Baseball, softball, cricket or other bats
- Tennis, squash, or badminton racquets
- Fishing rods
- Swords used in Scottish dancing
- Oars
- Bo staffs, jo staffs, bokken, or other martial arts weapons
- Chessboards
- Spanners, saws, or other tools
- Garden spades

.

PART FOUR:
WEDDING BELLS

RINGING OF BELLS

T he sound of a bell is one of the purest sounds humans have created. From its origin as a mechanism for ancient Romans to call their servants, bells moved into churches, and the tradition of ringing church bells for weddings has spread worldwide from its origin in Europe. While in Celtic tradition church bells were rung before the ceremony to ward off evil spirits and to announce the wedding, in Scotland, wedding bells were rung as the couple exited the church after the marriage ceremony.

Whether or not you're marrying in church, the ringing of bells both small and large in celebration of your new life together (and to dispel negative energy) can still be a feature of your wedding.

Use the traditional church bells

If you are marrying in church that has bells, they may well be available for weddings. Talk to the wedding coordinator or clergy regarding what is on offer and what melodies are available. The possibilities will depend on the number of bells – the fewer the bells the simpler the melody.

Hire a mobile bell peal

A mobile bell service may be available for hire in your area. If so, a portable cathedral bell peal will be brought to your wedding, positioned outside the church, venue, or outdoor ceremony space, and played both before and after the ceremony.

Use a recording

Recordings of bell peals are readily available both on CD and in MP3 format that you can download to a smart phone or iPod. Although a recording may not be audible outside the building unless you use a PA system and amplifier with speakers both inside and outside, a recording will allow you to have the peal of bells you wish, regardless of where you choose to marry.

Hand bells

A hand bell choir/ensemble/team could provide the music for your recessional. You need to be aware that the majority of pieces composed for hand bell choirs run for about four minutes. However, in addition to purpose-composed pieces, some well-known musical compositions have been adapted for hand bells, for example, God of Grace and God of Glory by Paul Manz.

A Word of Caution: Make sure the format of any recording you download is compatible with the equipment that will be used to play it. For an iPod or smart phone you will need to ensure that available speakers will deliver an appropriate volume.

THE TRUCE BELL

The Truce Bell is a charming Irish tradition and a great ritual because it recognizes the reality of married life. Sometimes referred to as a 'makeup bell', the bell is presented to the couple after they have made their vows, and they are invited to give the bell a good loud ring while thinking lovingly of one another, the vows they have just made, and their future together. In a religious ceremony the celebrant (officiant) will bless the bell before it is presented. In a non-religious wedding, no blessing is incorporated which means that the bell can be presented by the celebrant or by another significant person.

I like to place this ritual at the end of the ceremony, just before the recessional, as it concludes the ceremony on a wonderful upbeat note.

A Word of Caution: You will want the ring to be heard – so do not buy one of those dinky little favor bells meant to put on the tables at the reception. Choose a bell that that will make a statement at the ceremony and have presence in your home afterwards. A dinner bell, even a school bell will be a much better choice. Think outside the square. One of my couples found on eBay an old bell from a navy ship that had had family significance, and another used a lovely crystal dinner bell the bride had inherited from her grandmother. It may take some time to find the ideal bell, so start your shopping early.

Example words for your Truce Bell

Your selections from the words below may be mixed, matched, and edited to create a truce bell ritual that is very personal to you. Where appropriate, substitute *union* or *partnership* for the word *marriage*. Even better, let the examples below inspire you to create your own truce bell ritual using the template in the Appendix.

1. Today _____ and _____ are deeply in love and completely in tune. Nevertheless, they also have a realistic outlook on married life, so in anticipation of the inevitable, they have chosen to incorporate an old Irish tradition in their ceremony.
   Celebrant hands the bell to the couple.
   Please give this bell a hearty ring while thinking loving and positive thoughts about your future together.
   Couple rings the bell
   _____ and _____, put this bell in a prominent place in your home to remind you of the vows you made today. If ever you should start to argue, either of you can ring the bell to call a truce, without any admission of fault. The sound of the bell will remind you of this day, by conjuring up happy memories will help you to remember what is important, and will therefore help you resolve your differences with compassion and with love.

2. It has long been customary for bells to be rung immediately after a wedding. Today _____ and _____ are domesticating that practice by ringing the Truce Bell, an Irish tradition. This bell will be kept in a prominent place in their home, and if ever they should start to argue, one or other of them can ring the bell to declare a truce without an admission of fault.

_____ *presents the Truce Bell to* _____ *and* _____, *inviting them each to give it a good hard ring while thinking loving thoughts about one another.*

3. Bells have traditionally been rung at the conclusion of weddings to announce and celebrate the marriage and to chase away all bad things. Today _____ and _____ have chosen to celebrate their Irish heritage by domesticating that practice and by ringing the Truce Bell. They will keep the bell in their home and if ever they should start to argue, either can ring the bell to declare a truce without an admission of fault, thereby taking the heat out of the argument. _____ and _____, please take this bell, *Celebrant (officiant) hands bell to them,* and each ring it loudly three times, while thinking about the vows you have just made. _____ *and* _____ *ring the bell.* And now both of you, take hold of the bell's handle together and together ring it three times to celebrate that you are united by your love and are setting out on your journey towards becoming a family. _____ *and* _____ *ring the bell together.*

SOUND BLESSINGS

Small bells, kazoos, or the simple clapping of hands can accompany your recessional, harking back to the old belief that making noise chases away evil spirits. Guests often spontaneously break into applause as you walk back up the aisle, and where. Guests often spontaneously break into applause as you walk back up the aisle, and where your ceremony venue will not allow a toss of any sort, party poppers, kazoos, or the more genteel sound of tinkly bells can serve as a sound blessing.

Attach explanatory tags to them to ensure that the guests use them at the right time.

It will also be necessary to attach at least one length of ribbon to small bells to make the easier to grasp and to ring.

Ask you your celebrant (officiant) to cue the guests to start ringing their bells just before the recessional starts and to continue until the entire bridal party has exited. The tinkle of small bells will not drown out your recessional music but will add to the excitement.

For kazoos and party poppers you can safely leave the guests to their own devices as the sound will be intermittent.

PART FIVE:
TOSSES

WHAT IS A WEDDING TOSS?

A wedding toss is a wonderful way for guests to participate in, and add to, the finale to your ceremony or reception. A toss will also enhance the group photograph.

Showering newly married couples with the fruits of the earth (grains or flowers) is a very old custom that dates at least as far back as ancient Egypt, Greece, Rome, and parts of the Middle East.

Originally a fertility rite, the wedding toss symbolizes the hopes and wishes of the wedding guests that the couple will be blessed with fertility, prosperity, and abundance in their marriage. At different times and in different places wheat, corn, rice, nuts, flowers, and petals have been used because this custom that has evolved over the centuries to reflect the seed or grain common in the area together with local or current norms and expectations. Flowers are included because they were understood to carry the promise of fruit and therefore they too became associated with fertility.

In England the bride carried ears of wheat or wore a chaplet made of wheat and guests tossed ears of wheat and corn over her as she left the church. Guests and bystanders would pick up the kernels and eat them for luck and prosperity.

The use of rice as a substitute for wheat in English and American weddings dates from the 1870's. A certain John Jeaffreson documented the change, writing that his friend, Mr Moncure Conway, had described a wedding in London *"when rice was poured of the head of the bride"* and went on to note that the couple were *"English people, moving in the middle rank of prosperous Londoners".* No doubt, the fact that rice is white, smooth, and has had the husk removed and therefore is removed from its "rustic" origins, led to the substitution. In Victorian England *genteel* was the watchword

In Germany, it was believed that the couple would have as many children as the grains of rice that remained caught in the bride's hair. In Italy guests tossed confectionery, specifically sugar-coated nuts, (from which the word confetti derives).

Paper confetti was the first non-organic substitute for rice. The blowing of bubbles and the waving of sparklers are modern a twist on this tradition. However, rose petals remain a popular choice. If placed in decorative cones and tucked into the chair sashes, or placed in a decorative bag and hung on the chairs, they can do double duty as decorations.

A toss should not be thrown *at* the couple but rather thrown *up* above them, so that symbolically the blessing floats down from above. This reduces the need for the couple to duck, which compromises photographs.

It would be wise to consult with your venue before making any decisions. Some venues impose a total ban on tosses, citing the cost of cleaning and the risks associated with petals, seeds, and grains. They may charge a hefty clean-up fee if you ignore the ban. Others may allow biodegradable tosses, but some may ban fresh petals due to potential staining of carpets or risk of guests slipping and falling. If a toss is allowed, ensure the venue provides the specific of the permission in writing to avoid any disputes.

SCHEDULING YOUR TOSS

Once you have ascertained your wedding venue's policy regarding tosses, the next decision to make is when to schedule your toss.

For the ultimate finale to your wedding ceremony, the aisle toss ticks all the boxes. If, however, your ceremony is being held indoors in a church, chapel, or other indoor venue, your only option may be the traditional time for a toss – as you exit the building.

A Word of Caution: If you are exiting into a public space, check local littering laws before making the final decision about your toss.

HOW TO ENSURE A SUCCESSFUL WEDDING TOSS

Ensuring a successful wedding toss requires consultation with your venue and your photographer, selection of a toss that is appropriate to the venue, preparation, and coordination. Taking care of these aspects will ensure a successful wedding toss that your photographer will be able to capture for posterity in photographs that express the exuberance of the moment.

Weight counts

The lighter the individual piece of the toss is the better the toss will float and the longer it will remain airborne. Heavier items fall faster, lighter more slowly. The longer the toss remains in the air the better chance your photographer and your guests with cameras will have of capturing great images.

Visualize the moment

If you have scheduled your toss for your recessional, visualize when you want the toss to occur. Do you want your guests to toss as you approach them, so that the toss is sparser but continues for the whole of your walk down the aisle, or do you want everyone to toss at the same time, punctuating a particular moment? Discuss this with your photographer.

Rehearse

Ensure that your wedding rehearsal includes the toss (without actually throwing anything), so that your bridal party knows exactly what to expect. In addition, encourage those members of your wedding party who will be moving among the guests before the bride arrives to talk to your guests about their role in the toss and when it will occur.

Nominate leaders

Ask selected close friends to take the lead. Brief them thoroughly so that they can be sure to toss at the right time, giving the rest of your guests the cue to follow suit.

Prepare your guests

Include a note with your invitation or send an email a few weeks before your wedding to alert guests to venue policy regarding tosses. If you are having a toss, tell them that you will be providing what is needed for a toss that complies with that policy and include some specific instructions as to when the toss will occur.

Ensure everyone has a toss when it is needed

Place the bubble bottles or petal cones, envelopes, or bags where guests will be sure to see them. Add a sign to alert guests to pick one up. Alternatively have someone hand the tosses to guests, or place them on seats.

Ask adults to supervise children

Children may become overexcited and throw their toss prematurely. Encourage adults to keep custody of the petals or bubbles until the last moment.

Provide instructions

Add a tag or label to your petal cones or toss bags, envelopes, or sachets detailing as to when and how you would like guests to shower you with the contents. Include a few words about what the toss consists of and what it symbolizes.

OUT-OF-FAVOR TOSSES

The traditional tosses, confetti and rice, have fallen out of favor because, to reduce costs, churches and wedding venues now ban them.

Confetti

Confetti is made of brightly lightweight paper cut into tiny pieces, or into shapes such as lucky horseshoes or wedding bells, although generations of brides also saved the contents of office hole-punches for use on their wedding day.

Paper confetti may be purchased in regular commercial packaging or in customized boxes or containers designed to match the wedding theme or color scheme. To add fragrance to paper confetti spread it out on baking paper, mist with perfume, and allow to dry before packaging.

However, the very qualities that make confetti perfect for a wedding toss - it is small and light and therefore floats beautifully when thrown – also create problems. It spreads far and wide, gets into every nook and cranny, and requires a great deal of effort to clean up. Outdoors not even vacuuming will get it out of the lawn or flowerbeds. As a result, most wedding venues no longer allow the throwing of paper confetti, and the era of paper confetti appears to be coming to an end.

.Confetti companies are trying to fight this by producing environmentally friendly paper confetti that dissolves when it gets wet. Although eco-confetti will disappear completely the first time it rains, your venue may still fine you if you use it, so it would be advisable to confirm whether your venue allows it. Also, the very properties that make it biodegradable makes it prone to adhere to bare skin with even a slight sheen of perspiration. Photographs of your happy faces with multicolored patches on them may not be something you will appreciate in the years to come.

Rice

Churches, reception venues, and local authorities usually ban the throwing of rice. However, possibly because the real reason they do so – risk minimization – does not grab the imagination, there is a widespread belief that the ban is in place to protect birds, which will explode if they eat uncooked rice.

This is a myth, but a regularly repeated myth. Indeed, uncooked regular rice expands by a third when moistened, whereas bird seed expands by 40%. Uncooked rice is no more harmful to birds than birdseed or the rice they may feed on in the field. Indeed, many migrating species of birds depend on winter-flooded rice fields to build strength for their return to their northern breeding grounds.

On the other hand, humans are at real risk of harm. Uncooked rice on floors and walking surfaces, particularly hard wooden, marble, stone, concrete, and tiled surfaces, poses a danger both to guests and staff because it puts them at risk of slipping on it and falling, and to the church, proprietor of the venue, or the local authority because it puts them at risk of being sued.

Birdseed

Nonetheless, the banning of rice tosses has created a link in the mind of the public between rice and harm to birds, and given rise to promotion of birdseed as an alternative. Unfortunately, birdseed presents the same risk in regards to injuries to guests from slipping and falling. In addition, there is the added risk of the sharp parts of many seeds injuring eyes.

Further, there is no such thing as generic birdseed. Different species of birds will feed on different types and sizes of seeds. Birdseed designed for exotic caged birds is not suitable for wild bird. The wild birds native to the location of your wedding *may* eat the birdseed toss if it was thrown on lawn, but what is more likely to happen is that some of the seeds will germinate, and, because bird seed is a combination of seeds for plants that are rarely part of normal garden planting, a weed problem arises.

Finally, though this may seem to be stating the obvious, birdseed attracts birds. Imagine a birdseed toss in a city with a large pigeon population that has no fear of humans. The bride, groom, and the guests would be unlikely to escape without catching bird droppings in their hair and on their clothes, and frenzied birds swooping and diving are guaranteed to ruin any attempt at taking happy, relaxed, photographs of the couple.

Glitter and sequins

A fairly recent addition to the toss repertoire, glitter and sequins belong on this list. Both are difficult to clean up. Glitter is impossible to get rid of. It sticks to everything, and should never be thrown at or over a person because of the very real danger of eye damage. Glitter is metallic and sharp and can scratch the surface of the eye, causing painful damage to the cornea. Sequins are a hazard underfoot on hard surfaces, and likely to cause guests to slip and possibly fall.

ROSE PETALS

R oses are symbolic of love, and scattering rose petals over a newly married couple a visual representation of the blessing of family and friends. A rose petal toss raises the romantic temperature of your recessional, adds a touch of luxury, and creates amazing photo opportunities.

Rose petals for tosses come in three varieties – fresh, freeze-dried, and artificial, usually referred to as silk petals though they are generally made of artificial rather than natural fibers. Each type of petal has its benefits and its draw-backs, which need to be considered in order to arrive at the best choice for your needs.

Fresh, freeze-dried, or silk?

Whether you will be using the petals indoors or outdoors, the policy of the venue, personal preference, and your budget will drive your decision as to which type of petals will best meet your needs.

For outdoors both fresh and freeze-dried petals are appropriate because they are natural and biodegradable. For indoors freeze-dried or silk rose petals are more appropriate because they are easier to clean up, do not stain if they are kept dry, and are less slippery than fresh petals.

Fresh rose petals:

- If you purchase petals rather than whole roses, fresh rose petals are most expensive of the three types because you will be paying for the labor of removing the petals from the roses. To save, buy bunches of short-stemmed roses and delegate the de-petaling. To save, buy bunches of short-stemmed roses and delegate the de-petaling to friends or family members who can make themselves available to complete this task a few hours before the ceremony starts.
- Have a rich softness missing from the other types
- Are biodegradable
- Must be obtained on the day of use because they lose their freshness fast, particularly in hot or humid weather or if the roses were on their last legs before being de-petaled,
- May not be visibly bruised by handling and packaging
- Can be difficult or impossible to obtain at some times of the years, such as around Valentine's Day, or in mid-winter
- Can stain fabrics, carpets and flooring
- Can be slippery.

Freeze-dried rose petals

- Are the mid-price petals, not as expensive as fresh but more expensive than silk
- Are a long lasting alternative to fresh petals, having the look and feel of fresh petals
- Are a healthy option as any bacterial or fungal infestation is eliminated by the drying process
- Can be ordered and received several weeks before the wedding, but, as but they fade over time, especially if exposed to light and humidity, avoid having them delivered too far ahead of the wedding day
- Are lighter than fresh or artificial petals and therefore take longer to float through the air, thus increasing the chance of great photographs

- Are less likely to stain or cause guests to slip and fall, however, if it is raining they will rehydrate, increasing the possibility that they will cause stains and become slippery.

Artificial rose petals

- Generally the least expensive of the three options
- You get what you pay for with silk rose petals. Cheap silk petals can be almost transparent, look cheap, feel thin, and all the same size. Better quality silk rose petals will vary in size and won't be transparent. Look for petals made of a microfiber peach silk, giving them the texture and the weight of real rose petals.
- Will never decay, so you can obtain them well ahead of your wedding date.

Rose petal cannons

An exciting alternative to a hand-thrown petal toss are rose petal cannons. These are a spectacular but more expensive option. A simple twist of the base creates a whoosh of air and freeze-dried or silk rose petals are projected up to 12ft (4 meters) in the air. Two strategically placed people, each with a rose petal cannon to set off at this point, can either replace the rose petal toss by the guests or enhance it.

When adding a rose petal cannon to the guest rose petal toss choose paler petal colors for the guests and brighter petals shot from the cannons for a petal toss that pops.

Consider also pausing half way along the aisle during the recessional to share a second kiss. This emphasizes the love between you and provides a provides wonderful photo opportunity.

A Word of Caution: Some suppliers suggest that you can soften freeze-dried petals before use by opening them night before the wedding and exposing them to the air, or by placing them in the bathroom while taking a shower and that this will make them softer and more pliable (but not as soft as fresh petals). The longer the petals are exposed to humidity the softer they will become and the brighter darker colored petals will become. But be aware, softening petals this way can make them more slippery and more likely to stain, and will make them heavier, so that they will be less effective in your toss because they will descend more quickly than drier petals.

OTHER PETAL TOSSES

W hile rose petals are the more usual choice, they are by no means the only choice for your petal toss. If you are marrying in winter or close to Valentine's Day when prices rise and supply may be made more difficult by the high demand for roses, you may wish to consider alternatives, either on their own, or to mix with rose petals.

Companies that market freeze-dried petals continue to expand the range of petals available, recently adding delphinium and larkspur blossoms to allow you to add an all-natural *something blue* touch to your toss. The advantage of using freeze-dried petals is two-fold:

- the petals are much lighter than fresh petals because the process removes moisture, and therefore freeze-dried petals float through the air more slowly than fresh petals
- freeze-drying extends the season when the petals are available.

Some of the more common alternative petal tosses include bougainvillea, hydrangea, and lavender. Whole button chrysanthemums and jasmine blossoms are growing in popularity, and tiny individual flowers of baby's breath are light, inexpensive, and highly symbolic. You can also create your own unique petal mix for your toss.

Baby's breath

Making a come-back for flower girl bouquets and head wreaths, baby's breath is both visually and symbolically perfect for a toss. In the Victorian language of flowers it means *everlasting love*. It works particularly well when mixed with other flowers. It also dries easily. Just hang upside down in a warm dry place for a few days.

Bougainvillea

Bougainvillea "petals" (to be accurate, bracts), are lighter than rose petals and when thrown linger in the air longer than any other type of petal. This ensures that even the slowest photographer will get a picture. Bougainvillea comes in a wide range of bright and pastel colors, including white, and the petals are available for many months of the year. In warmer areas you may be able to source them at no cost from the gardens of family and friends.

Button chrysanthemums

The flower symbolism of chrysanthemums is abundance, hope, and wonderful friendship. The Japanese put a single chrysanthemum petal in the bottom of a wine glass to sustain a long and healthy life.

Carnations

The ragged petals of carnations, which in the Victorian language of flowers symbolize pure love, are a nice contrast with smooth rose petals for a mixed petal toss. At one time carnations were believed to have aphrodisiac qualities and therefore became linked with fertility. Their spicy clove aroma enhances the toss experience for your guests.

Cosmos

While not yet readily available in freeze-dried form, if you are planning a spring or summer wedding cosmos is worth the effort it will take to track down a source. Choose it for the rich color it will add to your toss - every shade of yellow, through orange to red, pink, and plum - and for its romantic meaning -- *joy in love and in life*. wide

For a fragrant toss, consider chocolate cosmos, which, as its name suggests, has an incredible chocolate fragrance.

Hydrangeas

Hydrangeas are available freeze-dried in a range of colors, including green. Though there are differences of opinion as to the symbolic meaning of this flower, the one that is most appropriate to weddings is that it represents any wish that is sincerely heartfelt.

Jasmine

Of all the flowers used in tosses, the jasmine has the strongest fragrance reflecting its symbolic meaning of sensuality, grace, and elegance. The flowers are used whole for tosses, and therefore you may wish to consider using it in a mixed toss rather than have a toss that consists solely of jasmine.

Lavender

In the language of flowers lavender represents love, loyalty, and devotion, and the color lavender symbolizes spirituality, creativity, mindfulness, and of spiritual connection with others, so using lavender buds for your petal toss adds more than fragrance and color. Lavender, the plant, comes in many more colors than lavender, the color. The flowers can be white, blue, pink, or purple. Strictly speaking, when you use lavender for a toss you are using buds, not petals. However, if you choose to mix lavender with other petals you may wish to use flower heads rather than individual buds. Lavender and rose petals have long been regarded to be a natural pairing. Cleopatra is reputed to have used a fragrance that incorporated both rose and lavender to seduce both Julius Caesar and Mark Anthony.

Peonies

In the language of flowers the peony symbolizes happy marriage. Although the choice of flower color is more limited in the peony than in the rose, these large, showy blooms are popular wedding flowers and now are available as freeze-dried petals.

HERB TOSSES

Herbs have been associated with weddings, and specifically with good wishes and blessings for the couple, for thousands of years. In ancient times, herbs were used in garlands and wreaths. In the Victorian era, herbs were mixed with petals and thrown as blessings for the happy couple as they left the church.

Today, as couples increasingly look for in-expensive and earth-friendly traditions to incorporate in their weddings, herbs are re-appearing as a romantic and aromatic alternative to rice, confetti, and more expensive flowers. Using herbs in your toss adds the color green, the symbolic color of wealth that is also associated with nature, fertility, abundance, good fortune, generosity and prosperity in all matters, healing, balance, vigor, renewal and growth.

Using herbs rather than flowers can also ensure that your toss is fit for human consumption, whereas some flower petals may carry residues of pesticides that may cause reactions in some guests. At certain times of the year most herbs do flower, producing small white or pink blossoms.

You can purchase fresh herbs at supermarkets, produce stores, or farmers markets. Dried herbs also work well, as long as the leaves are dried whole. You can dry herbs yourself if you have a cool, dry, place where you can suspend tied bunches head down, allowing them to dry naturally.

There are a number of other ways to home-dry herbs:

- Fill a box with sand (clean white sand available from a pet store is a good choice) place the herbs on the sand and sift more sand over until the herbs are completely covered.
- Place the herbs in the oven at a very low temperature until dry. The temperature should be the lowest temperature your oven can achieve in order not to cook the herbs. You will need to experiment
- Place the herbs in an airtight container and cover with silica gel crystals for an extended period.
- Use one of the home-food-drying appliances.

Avoid the bottles of dried herbs for sale in the spice aisle of your supermarket. Those herbs tend to be either ground or shredded into small particles which are too fine for an effective toss.

Good wedding herbs include:

Basil

This popular culinary herb symbolizes love and good wishes. The word *basil* derives *from* the Greek and means *king*. In Portugal, there is a tradition of presenting a basil plant to one's sweetheart on certain religious holidays. And in Italy it is commonly known as *kiss me, Nicholas!*

Marjoram

Legend has it that Aphrodite, the Greek goddess of love, created marjoram as a symbol of happiness. As a result, the Greeks crowned young couples with wreaths of marjoram, leading to an association with weddings.

Mint

This common herb symbolizes joy, wisdom, and virtue. It is probable that the hyssop of the Bible, like the modern hyssop, was a species of mint. In the Middle Ages mint was used to neutralize the "evil eye", so including it in your toss is suggestive of the willingness of your guests to protect your marriage.

Parsley

The ancient Greeks thought that parsley excited gaiety and appetite, so in the Victorian language of flowers it came to signify festivity. Both curly leaf and flat leaf parsley is suitable for a toss. Partial drying by hanging upside down in a warm dry place for a day or two will reduce its moisture content, making it easier to throw. If you can source parsley flowers from a home gardener, these will add a unique touch to your toss.

Rosemary

While rosemary has become associated primarily with remembrance, in ancient times this herb also represented love and fidelity and consequently it has been used in weddings throughout the ages. In Mexico, rosemary is grown as a good-luck charm.

Sage

Sage has long symbolized long life, good health, and domestic virtue.

Thyme

In Medieval times, ladies customarily embroidered a bee hovering over a sprig of thyme, symbol of courage, on the scarves they presented to their knights before combat. Given the association of bees with Cupid, Roman god of love, the symbolism is clearly romantic. An old superstition also suggests that thyme attracts money. According to legend, wild thyme was collected from the fields outside of Bethlehem to make a soft bed for Mary during the birth of Jesus.

To add an olde worlde element to your wedding, particularly if you are having a Medieval theme wedding, choose a mix of Parsley, Sage, Rosemary and Thyme, referring to the English ballad, *Scarborough Fair*. In the Middle Ages these herbs had as much romantic significance as red roses do to us today. They symbolize the virtues the singer wishes his true love and himself to have. When eaten, parsley was said to take away the bitterness of indigestion, and medieval doctors took this to mean in a spiritual sense as well as a physical one.

LEAF TOSSES

A romatic leaves can be an unusual, unexpected, and inexpensive alternative to petals, but even unscented leaves can make an attractive and inexpensive toss.

Good leaf tosses include:

Citrus leaves

Citrus trees are long lived. If properly cared for they can live for a century. Thus, the leaves convey positive symbolism for marriage. In English-speaking countries orange blossoms have been associated with wedding since Queen Victoria set the fashion by wearing a wreath of orange blossoms to symbolize fertility on her wedding day. Citrus leaves carry just as much meaning. The orange is one of a handful of plants that blooms and bears fruit at the same time, a powerful symbol of fertility. In Ancient China, orange blossoms were incorporated in a bride's costume as symbols of purity, chastity and innocence. Oranges, mandarins, tangerines and kumquats are given as symbolic gifts at Chinese New Year because of their symbolic association with good luck and abundance. Using the leaves of any of these types of citrus for your toss would therefore carry the same symbolism.

While using lemon or lime leaves for your toss might not be an obvious choice, it would be a meaningful one. Historically a symbol of longevity, purification, love and friendship, some sources also suggest that early Christians linked lemons with fidelity.

In ancient times the lime was the symbol of wedded love and conjugal bliss. As the story goes, the Greek gods Zeus and Hermes, messenger of the gods, were given shelter by Philemon the shepherd and his wife Baucis after being turned away from all other homes in the village. When they died, Zeus changed Philemon into an oak tree and Baucis into a lime tree.

Eucalyptus leaves

Eucalyptus is believed to bring good fortune to the couple, and, because of its use in medication, to ensure they enjoy good health together. Several varieties of eucalyptus leaves are suitable of a wedding toss. All are very aromatic and colours range from green-gray to blue-green. The round leaves of the *Silver Dollar* variety are particularly good to throw.

Fall (Autumn) leaves

For spectacular color, if you are lucky enough to live in an area where Mother Nature all serves up spectacular leaf color, and you are marrying in Fall, consider a toss of liquid amber, aspen, or other brightly colored leaves. Best of all, your neighbors will be more than happy to allow you to rake up their leaves.

While not herbs, three other plants make excellent additions to a herb or mixed toss because of their symbolism and attractive form.

Ivy Leaves

This easily grown plant, particularly *hedera helix*, beloved by brides for its heart-shaped leaves, was a popular addition to Victorian bridal bouquets and wreaths because it symbolizes of friendship, fidelity, and marriage. However, its role in weddings is far older. In

Ancient Greece ivy was sacred to Hymen, goddess of marriage and the wedding feast, and to Dionysus, god of wine and festivity.

Laurel leaves

In Ancient Greece and Rome the laurel was a symbol of honor. In the Victorian and Edwardian eras, laurel leaves were often engraved on narrow wedding rings, so that a wreath of laurels encircled the bride's finger. Laurel leaves are also used in a wide variety of cuisines, so are readily available as bay leaves in supermarkets and produce stores. When dried, laurel leaves have a slightly floral fragrance.

Myrtle Leaves

This traditional symbol of love, passion, and particularly marriage, is the ancient emblem of Aphrodite (Venus), goddess of love. The aromatic leaves will add fragrance to the toss.

Oak leaves

The ancient Romans believed that oak trees attracted lightning and this belief connected the oak tree to the sky god, Jupiter and his wife, Juno, the goddess of marriage. Thus, the oak is a symbol of conjugal fidelity and fulfillment. In Celtic tradition the oak symbolizes longevity, strength and endurance, generosity and protection, justice and nobility, honesty and bravery.

Olive leaves

Since Biblical times, the olive branch has been a symbol of peace. The olive is also strongly associated with Mediterranean cultures. In ancient times olive leaf wreaths were worn by brides and used to crown winners.

GRAINS AND LEGUMES

T he earliest tosses included grains common to the local area. While rice supplanted wheat in the 19th century, about the time the large white wedding became the norm, in rural areas of England ears of wheat continued to be featured in weddings into the early years of the 20th century.

Before deciding on one of the historically and symbolically significant grains or legumes for your toss, be sure that your venue will allow it.

Black eyed peas

Regarded to be a source of good luck in the South, black eyed are starting to appear in wedding tosses. Light, inexpensive, easy to find in any supermarket, and unusual, the dried peas unfortunately also share the characteristics of out-of-favor tosses. They are a slipping hazard on hard surface, they are difficult to clean up and they will germinate if they fall on lawns or in garden beds. On the other hand, if you are able to use them, pairing them with *I gotta feeling* by the Black Eyed Peas as your music, will add a very quirky twist to your recessional, but listen to the lyrics first. Some may think that they are a bit risqué. If black will not go well with your wedding color scheme, look for the variety that has pink eyes.

Corn

If you plan to use corn, choose parched corn. It is lighter and it will not germinate. However, it is a hazard underfoot and not easy to clean up, so check with your

Rice

Because of its romantic associations, if you are lucky enough to be able to use rice for your toss, and can safely do so, go for it. Guests understand it, and will appreciate the tradition behind it. Choose the more rounded medium grain rice over long grain rice which is more likely to hang around in your hair. Alternatively, reconstituted designer wedding rice (it is heart-shaped, water soluble, and smells like sugar cookies) is available.

A Word of Caution: If you are going to use regular rice, do not waste your money on 'wedding rice'. It is no different from the rice you buy in the supermarket, so you will be paying a huge premium for some fancy packaging. Do a little homework as to how much rice you'll need (i.e. how many cups of rice and how much that will weigh), purchase rice in the largest bag you can find (and it does come in huge bags), and package yourself for a fraction of the cost..

Wheat

Grains of wheat are an eco-friendly toss with a very long history. The toss of choice for many farming couples, it is light. However, it may be banned by your venue.

MIXED TOSSES

When it is not possible to obtain a sufficient quantity of a particular petal to meet your needs you could use a mixed toss. A mixed toss also allows you to bulk out your chosen toss with inexpensive choices in order to keep costs down. For a half-and-half toss, mix any two types of petals in equal quantities by volume. Good combinations are rose petals and jasmine, rose petals and lavender, or bougainvillea and hydrangeas.

For a more varied mix, choose four to six different flowers and herbs, choosing them to symbolize the specific blessings you hope for your marriage. While many herbs have leaves of similar sizes to flower petals, where the leaves are tiny, such as in thyme, rather than stripping the individual leaves off the stems clip tiny sprigs of similar size to the petals in your mix to ensure that the mix doesn't separate in the cone or bag.

For balance in a mixed toss mix equal quantities by volume of four different petals and/or herbs and then add an equal amount of rose petals (for example one cup each of carnation petals, lavender, jasmine flowers and sage leaves and 4 cups of rose petals. You can top off each cone with a few ivy leaves (for friendship), button chrysanthemum heads (for abundance) or olive leaves (for peace).

SEEMED LIKE A GOOD IDEA AT THE TIME

O ccasionally one hears about toss choices that just want you to shake your head and ask *'What were they thinking?'* Specifically, any toss material that is, or has the potential to become sticky, melt, or stain fabrics should be avoided. Throwing food of any kind will invite guests to think "Food Fight". And, in addition to normal clean-up issues, there is the possibility that any pieces missed in the cleanup will attract vermin.

I would strongly advise avoiding the following.

Oatmeal
Eco-friendly, light, smells good, and won't stain, but is very dusty, which won't make anyone wearing a dark suit (which generally means every male present) and will be slippery underfoot on hard surfaces. It is hard to clean up, the slightest bit of moisture will turn it into a porridge-like mess, and it will attract rats, mice, and cockroaches.

Popcorn
Yes, it is light. Yes, it will float nicely. Yes, it can be prepared and packaged ahead of time. But, humidity could make it go soft. On hard surfaces it will be a slipping and falling hazard underfoot. On carpet it could be ground into the carpet fibers by your guests' feet.

And small children will be tempted to pick it up off the floor and eat it, opening them to risk of tummy bugs.

Silly String

It is not only hard to clean up, it can stain and leave a bright spot of colored ink or foam from the string. On fabric, it has been known to permanently mark or remove paint from automobiles, and partly dissolve some varieties of wallpaper.

Sprinkles

Though the symbolism of having your guests shower you with sweet icing is charming and references the ancient custom of tossing candy or sweet fruits over the couple to ensure fertility, sprinkles must be kept completely dry. Humidity, perspiration, or rain will cause the food coloring in colored sprinkles to run, staining any fabric the sprinkles touch. Although white sprinkles avoid the staining problems created by rainbow or colored sprinkles, your bridal party, and any guests in the line of fire, will not be happy about needing to pick melted sugary sprinkles out of their hair or off their clothing and the venue wouldn't be happy about foodstuffs being ground into the carpet. Sugar also attracts wasps, bees, flies, and other even less desirable pests.

PRESENTING YOUR TOSS

Petal tosses are usually presented in individual petal cones which are placed for guests to take as they enter or exit the ceremony venue, handed to guests, or placed on their seats.

However, there are multiple other ways of presenting your toss. You can package the toss in organza favor bags, muslin or calico bags, in cellophane bags, or in glassine envelopes. You can present the toss in open baskets for guests just to take a handful, or you can provide one or more DIY toss filling stations.

Petal Cones

Cones are a popular choice because they are easy to use, requiring use of only one hand and a simple underhand tossing motion.

There is a wide choice of petal cones available commercially, and it is possible to buy cones already filled with fresh or freeze-dried petals, however it does not require a great deal of skill to fashion your own. Cones are just a piece of paper rolled so that one end is closed (at the point) and the other end is open. All you need to know is that you start at one side of the sheet of paper and roll it towards the side of the sheet that is at a 90º angle, that is, roll the right corner in towards the left corner. The pointed end of the cone lies at the corner where the two sides meet. If you prefer a flat end rather than a point, simply fold over the pointed end and tape or glue it into place.

You can use rectangular or square sheets of paper both of which will give you a cone with a higher back suitable for threading a ribbon loop through to hang on the chairs or space to print the names of the couple, date of the ceremony, or instructions for when the toss is to occur.

Choose thicker paper so that your cones have some body. Translucent vellum, flocked, embossed, or flower pressed paper add a classy touch to petal cones. Pages of old books or sheets of music can speak to your personal interests or reflect the theme of your wedding.

Round paper doilies, cut in half, are easy to use and, because of their built-in perforated border, require nothing more than a sticker, or a wax seal to hold them together. Alternatively, you can close the cones by using concealed double-sided tape or a hot glue gun and decorate them with stamped images complementing the color scheme of the wedding. Doilies are available in white, silver and gold from most outlets, as well as pastel colors from some specialist survivors. They are also easy to spray paint using acrylic paint. You can make spray the whole doily or just add the color to the perforated edge. The finished size of the cone top to tip is the radius of the doily, thus a 12 inch doily will make two 6 inch cones. To roll, mark the half way point on the cut side as a guide to where the point will lie.

Cellophane Bags

Cellophane and glassine bags are available in a wide range of different sizes. They're cheap and sturdy, and being transparent. show off the toss to good effect and allow you to print decorative designs, your names, the date and instructions on a piece of paper almost as big as the bag. Cut the paper just slightly narrower than the bag in order to ensure a snug fit and short enough to allow the top inch and a half of the bag to be gathered and tied with a ribbon, or folded over and secured with a sticker. If you would like to hang the bags from the chairs use a hole punch to make two holes through all four layers of the folded section and thread a loop of ribbon through, tying it off with a bow.

Drawstring Fabric Bags

Drawstring bags are a popular choice for lavender buds, rice, and other grain tosses where you need to restrict the amount that can be tossed by any one person to a small handful in order to minimize the potential for injury. However, they do not work particularly well for petals unless the opening is large enough to allow a guest to take a handful of petals out of the bag. Bags require two free hands, so can prove a challenge to female guests who may be juggling a purse and a wrap as well as the toss.

Choose organza bags, available in a wide range of colors, or cotton or muslin which you can decorate by stamping with your monogram, a wedding design, or words from your vows. Do not double-knot the drawstrings. Just pull the drawstrings tight so guests can get to the toss quickly and easily.

Boxes

Boxes work relatively well for all tosses. Because the top is open guests can easily transfer the toss from the box to their hands, or they can toss direct from an open box using a similar underhand toss to that required for a petal cone.

PRACTICAL CONSIDERATIONS

You will need to ascertain how many containers of tosses you will need, and to calculate the volume of the toss you will need to fill them all. You will also need to identify appropriate sources, arrange for delivery or collection, and delegate helpers to package the tosses ready for the ceremony.

To ensure your tosses are as fresh and lovely as possible, cut the stems diagonally and stand them into cool water. Keep them in the water until you are ready to package the toss.. Strip the petals as close to the wedding time as possible, definitely no earlier than the morning of the wedding.

If using dried petals ignore any instructions to open and expose to the air to allow the petals to soften. Instead, keep the package sealed until the last possible moment so the petals will remain as dry and light as possible and will therefore take longer to drift to the ground after being tossed.

Fill cones or bags the day of the wedding, preferably as close to the time of the wedding as is practical. This is a task you can and should delegate

Calculating what you need

If presenting the toss already packaged in a cone or bag, you'll need about ½ cup of fresh or freeze-dried flower petals or petal/herb/leaf mix per cone/bag. For silk rose petals allow 12 per guest.

For confetti, rice, or grain tosses, that you are presenting in smaller cones or bags, about ¼ cup is sufficient.

If presenting a petal toss in a basket for guests to take handfuls themselves, allow ¾ cup per guest to allow for spillage and larger handfuls..

How to remove petals from flowers

Pull the petals gently from the flowers and drop them in a broad flat container, such as a basket, so the petals are neither crushed nor bruised.

Roses

Ensure that the roses are slightly soft. With one hand hold the rose stem up close to the base of the rose. With your other hand cup the rose head and carefully pull the head to one side. You will find that all the petals will come off together with minimal damage, leaving the core of the rose (the stamens) attached to the stem.

Carnations and daisies

Gently grasp the flower stem near the head in one hand. Grasp several petals between the thumb and fingers of the other hand and carefully pull out the petals.

DISTRIBUTING YOUR TOSS

Getting the toss into the hands of your guests is critical to ensuring that it all goes smoothly. For a recessional toss you need to make sure that everyone has a filled container before the ceremony starts, so you can employ a number of strategies:

- Have someone hand a toss to each of the guests on arrival
- Put baskets of the tosses at strategic positions near the entrance with a sign inviting to guests to serve themselves.
- Hang an individual toss on each chair
- Tuck a petal cone into the chair sash
- Place a bag or envelope on each seat
- For a standing wedding have ushers or others circulate through the guests as they are gathering or where there is a pause between the pronouncement and kiss, and the recessional while a formal signing of documents takes place.. This is a good job for older children.
- For a smaller, more casual wedding, set up wedding toss stations near the entrance to the ceremony space and invite guests to mix their own toss and fill a container.

For a toss as the couple exits the church or other indoor space, position ushers on either side of the door so people can take either a container filled with the toss or a handful of petals as they make their way outside.

Where your toss is scheduled to take place during the shooting of group photographs almost rose petals are the preferred toss. Have one or more people circulate among the guests with petal cones or an open basket or box inviting them to take a handful of petals as they gather for the photograph.

When distributing petal cones from baskets it is a good idea to suggest that the person doing the distributing starts from the center of the basket and works their way to the outside rim of the basket to maintain balance.

TOSS TAGS

Attach a tag or label to each bag or envelope containing the toss, or to each bubble bottle. On petal cones and cellophane or glassine envelopes the label can do double duty - holding the cone together as well as providing instructions, keeping the envelope closed, or serving as a decorative element. If using drawstring bags punch a hole in the tag and thread one of the drawstrings through the hole. Then pull the drawstrings tight and tie a single knot to hold the tag in place.

Use simple language, such as

- *Shower us with your blessings and these petals as we walk back down the aisle*
- *Bless us with your love tossed from above*
- *Throw these petals high when we walk by*
- *Toss these to congratulate us as we walk back up the aisle*

Or add a verse, such as

- *With a great big smile*
  As they walk down the aisles
  Blow these bubble kisses
  over the new Mr & Mrs

- *To ensure _____ and _____ exit with flair*
  Toss these pretty petals high in the air

- *Roses for love, Lavender for devotion*
  Please toss high in the air
  Over the newly-married pair
  While creating a commotion.

- *When the ceremony is done*
  and we head for the door
  Toss these petals up high
  As we pass by.

- *When we exit as a pair*
  Toss these high in the air
  So that your good wishes and love
  Shower down on us from above.

TOSSING TECHNIQUE

The success of your toss depends largely on the technique used to throw or deliver what is being tossed. The rule of thumb is that petals, grains, or confetti should be tossed above you and slightly ahead of you so it floats down onto you where you are, not where you've just been.

An underhand toss, aiming the petals high above the heads of the couple, works well. An overhand throw angles the petals on a down-ward trajectory, or straight for the couple's faces, neither of which technique makes for good photographs.

Petal cones facilitate an underhand toss straight out of the cone. But this might not come naturally as instinctually, and as a result of a lifetime of being socialized that throwing anything at another person is unacceptable, guests might hold the cones high and empty the petals onto the couple's heads. Overcome this by attaching a label.

An instructive label attached to bags and envelopes will alert guests to the need to pour the petals into their hands before tossing with an underhand movement.

TURN THE TABLES

While the traditional wedding toss involves the guests showering the couple, weddings are also an opportunity for the couple to show their gratitude to their families and friends in a fun and exuberant fashion.

A spectacular, and unexpected, way to do this is for the bride and groom to reverse tradition and shower their guests with petals rather than vice versa. As you start down the aisle, leave the bouquet behind in the custody of one of your bridesmaids, or hand it to one of the mothers, then each grab a basket of petals and shower your guests as you go. Share spontaneous words of appreciation and joy with your guests to ramp the excitement of the moment up even more.

Alternatively, you may choose to provide two petal cannons and have your bridal party hold them at a 45 degree angle pointing over the heads of your guests. Coordinate letting them off with your first step down the aisle, so that your photographer captures you walking between your guests with petals floating down on their heads on either side of you.

BUBBLES

Walking back down the aisle through a cloud of bubbles adds an element of playfulness to your recessional and makes for magical photographs. For same-sex couples bubbles have additional symbolism because they incorporate all the colors of the rainbow, albeit subtly.

Bubbles are allowed by most churches and venues, though it is best to check as some impose a ban because of the possibility that carpet and fabric may be stained

A bubble toss works best if the bubbles are neither overly small nor sparse. Many of the small bottles of bubbles made specifically for weddings come with extremely small openings in the wand This restricts the size of the bubbles, makes it difficult to achieve a shower of bubbles, and requires a level of manual dexterity and hand-eye coordination that may be beyond children and older guests with arthritic hands. Where possible choose bubble bottles that include a flexible wand that opens wide when removed from the bottle creating larger bubbles.. You might also consider using a bubble machine placed about halfway down the aisle. But if you do, ensure that the machine is not visible in the aisle as that will compromise photographs and will create a hazard to those walking down the aisle.

Plan ahead to ensure an appropriate density of bubbles. Place the bubble containers in a prominent position so your guests will see them as they enter the church or ceremony space. Attach a large sign to the basket in which you've placed the bubble containers asking guests to take one and indicating when the bubble toss will occur. For example, *Please take one and shower us with bubbles and your blessings as we walk back up the aisle.* Ask your ushers to reinforce the message by talking guests through what is planned as they take their containers. Reinforce the message by adding a small tag to each container, for example *Blessing Bubbles for the end of the ceremony.* You could also include explicit instructions in your Program (Order of Service booklet).

In addition, ask your celebrant (officiant) to coordinate the bubble toss. He or she can do this by asking your guests to stand and crowd towards the aisle before you start your walk back up the aisle and to start blowing bubbles on a signal from the celebrant.

A Word of Caution: Bubbles eventually fall to the ground, so be careful if you are walking out on polished wood floors, or on marble, stone or granite surfaces or steps because the bubbles could make these slippery. If the detergent concentration is too high bubbles can stain delicate fabrics. If the bubble solution is old the bubbles will be tired and sparse. To ensure that your bubbles are fresh (which means the bubble wands will produce lots of large lively bubbles that glisten in the light) buy good quality bubble solution as close to your wedding date as possible and buy from from a reputable supplier with a high turnover. Test the solution by blowing some bubbles directly at a sample of the fabric of your wedding gown and bridesmaids gowns to check whether the solution will stain. If you do not have a sample of the fabric choose a section of the hem turn-up in an unobtrusive area inside the dress. Ensure that your guests blow the bubbles up over your heads rather than directly at you.

ALTERNATIVES TO TOSSES

The possibilities for alternatives to a petal or bubble toss are only limited by your imagination. Where your toss choices are limited by the policy of your ceremony or reception location, thinking outside the square can result in a very different toss that also meets the needs of the venue. Because these alternatives are easy to pick up, you will avoid clean-up fees.

Balloon Drop

If your venue will allow it, and the ceiling design facilitates it, organize a balloon drop for the moment when you kiss, or when you start down the aisle. Fill small latex balloons with air, not helium, and put them in a balloon net or bag designed for drops. You need to decide on how many and what size balloons in order to work out what size net you need to allow for a smooth and coordinated drop. Avoid large balloons. They may look spectacular but are likely to obscure faces in photos. You will also need to appoint someone to pull the rope to cause the drop.

Flags

Give your guests flags printed with your names, the date, a word or two of good wishes, or a jubilant exclamation (*Yay!*, *Hooray!*, or *They Did!*, for examples) to wave as you walk down the aisle.

Mini Beach Balls

Lightweight mini beach balls make a fun toss that will add an extra element of fun as they hit the ground and rebound.

Paper Airplanes

Provide paper airplanes made from lightweight paper for guests to throw into the air above your heads as you walk down the aisle.

Pom Poms

Imagine walking back up the aisle between enthusiastically shaken cheerleader pom poms in your favorite team's colors. Mini pom poms, available from craft stores, are light, colorful, fun, and difficult to clean up.

Ribbon Wands

Wands can be purchased or made very easily. All that you need is lengths of wooden dowel, a light saw to cut a notch in one end of dowel, and multiple lengths of ribbons to glue into the notch. This is an easy project that younger members of the family can help with.

Ribbon Wands with Bells

Add tiny bells to the top of the wand for a glint of gold or silver. To ensure that the tinkle of bells does not interrupt the ceremony, schedule distribution for the end of the ceremony, while you are signing the register and marriage certificate.

Streamers

Throwing of streamers from ship to shore and dock to ship was a "Bon Voyage" custom in the days before airline travel. Paper streamers are cheap to purchase, easy to throw, and a breeze to clean up because they are large. They also add an element of fun to your walk back up the aisle or departure from your reception that would be difficult to match with any other toss.

Sparklers

Sparklers make for a fantastic wedding finale when used to light your path as you leave the reception and head for your getaway car. They can also add a touch of magic to your recessional or to your exit from the ceremony venue after a twilight ceremony. However, because sparklers can pose a fire threat, you will need to ensure that your venue's insurers allow their use. You also need to manage the logistics to enable everyone to light their sparkler almost simultaneously. One way to do this is to create lighting stations on either side of your exit route. Place tiki torches or long sparklers in pots of soil placed at strategic intervals, delegate the ushers or other suitable people to light these, enabling your guests to light their sparklers quickly and efficiently.

Glow sticks

Where sparklers are banned, or if you want to add color to your after dark departure, consider using glow sticks. You may have to duck a bit, or suggest that your guests toss the glow sticks so they land on the path ahead of you. Your reward will be fantastic photos.

PART SIX:
TRANSITION/CONCLUSION RITUALS

WHAT IS A TRANSITION OR CONCLUSION RITUAL?

In addition to the recessional, there are a number of other rituals, some of them culture-specific, that mark the transition of a couple from single status to that of a married or committed couple. These rituals also signal that the ceremony has ended and create a bridge between the ceremony and what follows.

Releases

The releasing of balloons, butterflies, and doves represent the most recent evolution of the wedding toss. As the throwing of rice and confetti became less and less widely acceptable, commercial entities started to promote releases as an alternative that, because no detritus landed in the immediate vicinity, met with little opposition from churches and wedding venues.

However, as environmental and other concerns surface, more local and state authorities are regulating releases. In some places certain types of releases are banned by local authorities or prohibited by-law. In areas where releases are still allowed you may be required to provide proof that you have adequate liability insurance before a permit is issued.

It would be wise to ascertain what, if any, state laws or city or municipality regulations may apply before committing yourself to a release. Restrictions on species of butterflies, predators in the area, and limits on size of the release, together with the policy of the church or venue at which you are holding your ceremony may all impact on the viability of a release in your area.

Breaking the Glass

Possibly the most universally acknowledged Jewish wedding custom is the breaking of the glass by the groom at the end of the ceremony. Although it is a non-religious custom, no Jewish wedding ceremony is complete without it, and therefore it is a ritual that is routinely included, on the Jewish side of the equation, in inter-faith ceremonies.

Breaking the Vase

While apparently similar to the Jewish custom, the Italian tradition of a bride and groom breaking a vase at the end of the reception is symbolically completely unrelated.

Jumping the Broom

A ritual which has roots in a variety of cultures, jumping the broom has been particularly embraced by African-American couples. It is also common in Scottish and in pagan weddings.

BALLOON RELEASE

From ancient time humans have sent wishes and prayers skywards using smoke, incense, and, a recent innovation, helium-filled balloons. A wedding balloon release is usually structured as a wishing ritual that sends hopes and wishes for the couple's future happiness aloft. A balloon release may also be symbolic of the start of a journey that has endless possibilities.

Balloons allow one to write wishes, hopes or intentions on them. For example, you could write words such as *Love, Hope, Fidelity, Joy,* and *Happiness* as your wishes for yourselves and your marriage..

Although a balloon release can be carried out as a formal ritual, in the tradition of a dove release, balloon releases tend to be less formal than either butterfly or dove releases. This may be because subliminally we associate balloons with children's parties, New Year, and other free-flowing celebrations. There also tends to be wide variety in the words spoken to introduce a balloon release. Readings from books such as Dr Seuss *Oh, the places you'll go,* are commonly used in weddings to convey a sense of joy and exuberance.

Or, you can just give all of your guests a balloon and have them release them for a group photo, as you walk down the church steps, or as you walk through an informal guard of honor formed by your guests on either side of your path.

Before deciding to have a balloon release you should check local laws and by-laws. Some areas have banned latex balloon releases outdoors. Some have stringent restrictions on the number of balloons that may be released without a permit. As well as checking for specific legislation, it would be wise to check littering laws as some jurisdictions classify balloon releases as littering and may impose on-the-spot fines.

Because whole balloons are hazardous to both marine and land animals and birds, it is important to use only latex balloons and to ensure that the balloons will rise high enough to allow a combination of atmospheric pressure and low temperature to make them brittle. This is necessary to allow the balloons to fracture into small pieces that will float back to earth.

You should also take care to minimize both environmental impact and hazards to humans and to aircraft.:

- Use only biodegradable latex balloons filled with helium. Mylar balloons, or balloons with metallic ribbons attached, can cause power outages if they touch electrical lines. They can also pose a risk of electrocution if someone touches a metallic balloon or ribbon that is in contact with electrical wiring.
- Release no more than 10 balloons
- Fill the balloons shortly before they are to be released and make sure they are fully inflated.
- Avoid adding anything to a balloon. Clips, tags, cards, keys, or strings can add the very minimal amount of extra weight that will prevent the balloon rising high enough to fracture, so that it will return to earth intact, posing a threat to wildlife, which may mistake balloons for food for example confusing a balloon with a jellyfish and either choke or sustain a blockage in the animal's digestive or respiratory system, so that it either starves or suffocates. Even small fragments can cause similar problems in smaller animals and

birds. Any messages you wish to attach to the balloon can be easily and safely written on the balloons with a felt tip pen. An added benefit is that the messages will be visible in photographs.

Where latex balloon releases are prohibited, you may still be able to obtain permission to release eco-friendly paper balloons. These are soluble in water but do not hold helium for as long as a latex balloon. A Japanese invention, you will find numerous educational websites explaining how to make them from tissue paper or, if you wish to purchase, you will find them at stores selling Japanese paper and party goods. Some paper balloons come with biodegradable message tags and biodegradable string already attached. Cut the strings as short as possible to make sure that no bird or animal will become entangled in them.

You may also consider releasing balloons indoors where they will hover at ceiling height for the rest of the evening. With indoor releases you can be much less stringent about what you attach to the balloons. Releasing the balloons indoors enables you to attach ribbon tails, tags, or cards.

A dramatic alternative to releasing balloons is to give everyone a balloon and a pin and, when cued, everyone bursts their balloon, sending wishes skywards.

A Word of Caution: While environmentally friendly, many paper balloons do have a small amount of metal in them, so you should avoid releasing them near power lines, or where they might fall into areas where animals might eat them.

Example Words for your Balloon Release

Your selection from the words below may be mixed, matched, and edited, to create a balloon release that is very personal to you. Where appropriate, substitute *union* or *partnership* for the word *marriage.* Even better, let the examples below inspire you to create your own balloon release using the template in the Appendix.

1. In various ways people have always sent hopes and wishes skywards. Today we send our wishes on balloons. May _____ and _____ have a long and happy marriage filled with love, luck, lots of laughter.

2. Love leaves memories that none can take away. Today _____ and _____, with their family and friends, have made memories to last a lifetime, memories that they hold in their hearts as the balloons carrying their hopes and dreams for their marriage rise to the heavens.

3. _____ and _____ release these balloons in celebration of their marriage, the love they share, the love that has surrounded them all their lives, and the love that surrounds them today.

BUTTERFLY RELEASE

The association of butterflies with the soul or spirit is found in Greek mythology and in many cultures. The word *psyche*, which psychologists and others use to refer to the personality or innermost mind, that is, what makes an individual tick, comes from the ancient Greek word for soul. Psyche was Eros' (Cupid in Roman mythology) human lover. When Eros and Psyche are depicted together in frescoes and decorations on Greek and Roman pottery, butterflies often surround them.

Butterflies are commonly associated with transformation, however, the association of butterflies with lovers is far less widespread. In China two butterflies flying together are a symbol of love. In the United States, Canada, Australia, New Zealand, the United Kingdom and other western countries, butterflies are now regarded to be a symbol of love and of the beginning of a new journey and the release of butterflies symbolic of the journey just beginning for the newlyweds as they start their life together.

Monarch butterflies are the species of choice for releases because they fly slowly and are attracted to brightly colored clothes, and tend to hang around after being released. They are also attracted to the salt in perspiration, making it more likely that they will alight on your hand. All other species of butterflies tend to fly off more quickly.

You have two options for your release:

- Individual releases with one butterfly per small container (envelope or small triangular box), or
- A mass release from a single specially designed container.

If you choose to have a mass release, you will need to arrange for someone to transfer the butterflies from their individual shipping boxes to a larger release container.

To capture the attention of the guests and share the meaning of the release, it is usually introduced with a poem, reading, or announcement. The oft-repeated 'Native American Legend' that a butterfly carries wishes to the heavens is a recent invention of a butterfly breeding business. There is no credible association with Native American mythology.

Where you wish to include a religious element, the butterflies can be released with a prayer. You may wish to refer to the fact that the Spanish word for butterfly, *mariposa,* is a contraction of the phrase *la Santa Maria posa,* meaning the Virgin Mary alights/rests and include a prayer to the Virgin.

Butterfly releases are time and season sensitive. The destinations to which the butterflies may be shipped, and/or releases of butterflies may also be controlled by government regulations. With the exception of countries in continental Europe; butterflies destined for release are generally not permitted to be shipped across national borders. You will therefore need to source your butterflies from a breeder in your own country.

In the United States, Butterfly Farmers must have permits from the United States Department of Agriculture (USDA) to ship butterflies across state lines. Not all butterflies can be shipped into all states and Monarch butterflies may not be shipped across the Continental Divide.

The time of year may preclude your having a butterfly release. Breeders will not supply butterflies for release in the winter months. Butterflies also naturally rest at night and need time before sunset to find both food and shelter. They should therefore not be released early in the morning, at any time when the temperature is below 60 Fahrenheit (15.5 degrees Centigrade), in the hour leading up to sunset, at night, or when it is raining heavily. Nor should they be released indoors.

Reputable breeders will ship the butterflies with icepacks to ensure they remain in a state of hibernation and travel without stress. The farm-raised butterflies supplied for releases are newborns. They require a natural resting environment during shipping and in the period between delivery and release. They need to be handled carefully.

When your butterflies are delivered you should carefully follow the directions sent by the breeder. To ensure that the butterflies are ready to fly the instructions will suggest that they should be allowed to warm up to about 65 degrees Fahrenheit (18 degrees Centigrade), and that they should be exposed to indirect light in their containers over a period of approximately one hour immediately before they are released. Butterflies must never be left in a vehicle or other hot place.

A Word of Caution: Because there is concern that transporting and releasing butterflies that come from a different area and therefore a different gene pool may negatively affect the local population of that same species through introduction of new viruses or diseases, some of your guests may react negatively to a butterfly release. In addition, while phobias about butterflies are not common, a phobic guest could become hysterical. And don't forget that butterflies and bug sprays do not mix!

Example Words for your Butterfly Release

Your selection from the words below may be mixed, matched, and edited to create a butterfly release that is very personal to you. Where appropriate, substitute *union* or *partnership* for the word *marriage*. Even better, let the examples below inspire you to create your own butterfly release using the template in the Appendix.

1. The butterfly is a powerful symbol of transformation. Today, as _____ and _____ set out on their journey as husband and wife, they take with them the love and nurturing of their families and friends.

2. _____ and _____ invite you to join with them in expressing their joy by releasing butterflies, symbol of love and transformation.

3. Butterflies are powerful symbols of joy and of change. Because they alight briefly, delighting us with their beauty before taking flight again, they encourage us to savor the moment. For all these reasons _____ and _____have asked their bridal party to join them in a butterfly release to accompany a traditional Irish blessing.

May the wings of the butterfly kiss the sun

And find your shoulder to light on

To bring you luck, happiness and riches

Today, tomorrow, and beyond.

The butterflies are released one by one as the blessing is said

Example Program Notes for your Butterfly Release

Butterflies remind us that life can be both beautiful and fragile. _____ and _____ invite you to join with them in releasing butterflies at the end of the ceremony in celebration of their marriage.

DOVE RELEASE

C ouples choose to release doves for the symbolism of doves flying free and for the photo-opportunities the release offers. A dove release is rich in symbolism for a wedding because doves care for and protect one another and because they mate for life.. A dove release is therefore a ritual that celebrates the beginning of your marriage and expresses hopes for a long, faithful, and loving marriage. It is always conducted outdoors, so if you marry in church the release will take place at the end of the recessional, after you have exited the building.

You have two options for your wedding dove release:

- You can choose a hand release, where you each hold one dove and release them from your hands, or
- You can opt for a flock release (sometimes referred to as a flurry) in which a number of doves are released immediately after the bride and groom release two doves so that a large group of doves take flight.

It is usual to introduce the dove release with a poem, reading, or announcement to capture the attention of the guests and share the meaning of the release. However, unlike balloon or butterfly releases, dove releases tend to be tightly controlled by the professional handlers who may supply you with their preferred wedding release text in the expectation that you will use it. To make sure that the handler knows exactly when you want the doves to be released, share your text and get confirmation that the cues will be followed. Do not attempt to self-manage your dove release. An experienced professional handler who understands bird behavior and how to time the release for best effect will deliver optimum results for your photographer, for you, and for your guests.

Ethical dove release businesses will not supply birds to wedding held further away than 50 miles (80 kilometers) from their home loft. Nor will an ethical business supply doves in areas where predators such as hawks are prolific. They will also ensure that the release takes place in optimal conditions for the birds. This means that sufficient time will be allowed for the birds to be able to return home before dark. Birds released when it is too late in the day may be reluctant to come out of their baskets, defeating the purpose of the release and compromising the symbolism. A reputable business will stipulate in the contract that the release will be cancelled if the weather is bad and will return fees paid should conditions not be conducive to the release.

A Word of Caution: Use only specially bred and well-trained white homing pigeons supplied by an ethical business and accompanied by an experienced handler. Any other bird, including white 'Ring Neck' doves sold in pet stores should not be released as to do so is to condemn them to death in the wild.

Before committing yourself to the idea of a dove release, you should do two things:

- check with the authorities whether bird releases are legal in your area.
- Ensure that no-one present is phobic about birds. Bird phobias are relatively common, and a phobic guest could become hysterical.

Example Words for your Dove Release

Your selection from the words below may be mixed, matched, and edited to create a dove release that is very personal to you. Where appropriate, substitute *union* or *partnership* for the word *marriage*. Even better, let the examples below inspire you to create your own fire lantern release using the template in the Appendix.

1. Doves in flight represent joy, true love, and the security of knowing that home is where the heart is. _____ and _____ have chosen to celebrate their love and their union with a flight of doves.

2. Doves are powerful symbols of joy and fidelity. Because they mate for life, and return home after every flight, they remind us of the importance of loving companionship. _____ and _____ release these doves in celebration of their marriage and to honour *[insert names]* whose marriage they hope to emulate.

3. White doves symbolize peace, love, and life-long fidelity. To celebrate their marriage _____ and _____ have chosen to release white doves whose exuberant flight echoes the excitement with which they begin married life.

4. Jonas Salk reminds us that *Good parents give their children roots and wings - roots to know where home is and wings to fly off and practice what has been taught them.'* _____ and _____ have chosen to release doves to honor their parents to, celebrate the wings their parents gave them, and to acknowledge with gratitude the firm foundation, given them by their parents, which gives their relationship strength.

BREAKING THE GLASS

No Jewish wedding would be complete without the sound and sight of the groom stomping on a napkin-wrapped glass and the shouts of *Mazel tov* from the guests.

While it is not uncommon for wedding planners to advise substituting a light bulb in order to ensure that the first stomp would achieve the objective, traditionally the glass must be that used to drink from for the second blessing.

To protect everyone from potential injury, the glass is wrapped in a linen napkin or placed in a bag before the groom stamps down on it with his right foot. In egalitarian ceremonies, the bride joins the groom in breaking the glass.

For centuries a number of stories have circulated about the origin and meaning of the ritual, which first became popular about 800 years ago, but it seems that it has its roots in the Talmud, which recounts the occasion on which the breaking of an expensive glass was used to tone down a raucous wedding party. By the 14th century the interpretation was changing and the act of breaking a glass was held to memorialize the destruction of the Temple in Jerusalem.

Some commentators suggest that the breaking of the glass symbolizes the breaking of hearts in remembrance of that historical event. Others suggest that the custom owes its existence to medieval superstition when making a noise by shattering a glass was thought to ward off evil spirits and thus protect the marriage.

A modern interpretation is that, in addition to its role as a historical reminder, the breaking of the glass symbolizes the fragility of marriage and therefore serves to remind the couple that, with the support of family and friends, they must take care to carefully nurture their relationship.

A Word of Caution: While the old incandescent light bulbs may have been safe to break, modern energy efficient light bulbs can contain toxic components. It is therefore both safer and more authentic to use a thin wineglass. Avoid a shot glass because they are not only very sturdy, their small size can result in them getting 'lost' in the napkin so that groom may not be able to easily discern where the glass is and may stomp down on empty napkin.

BREAKING THE VASE

While the breaking of the glass by the groom customarily concludes a Jewish marriage ceremony, in Italian custom the couple stomps on a vase together at the end of the reception. They do their best to grind it into as many pieces as possible because the number of shards is believed to represent the number of happy years the couple will have together.

This custom was seen in the movie *When in Rome* starring Josh Duhamel and Kristen Bell, but as might be expected in a romantic comedy, the breaking didn't go to plan resulting in some hilarious attempts to smash the very large ceramic vase.

With the permission of your celebrant (officiant) you might include this ritual as the last act of your ceremony, immediately before the recessional..

JUMPING THE BROOM

Broom-jumping is a joyful transition ritual. Hand-in-hand the bride and groom move into married life by jumping over a decorated broom. Some couples jump the broom at the end of the ceremony and then continue walking back down the aisle. Others jump the broom at the reception.

Whatever your cultural heritage, the tradition of jumping the broom has been passed down orally, so there is no 'authorized' way of staging it. You can have your celebrant (officiant) signal your intention and preface the ritual with some well-chosen words of explanation. You can include a symbolic sweeping of obstacles out of your path. You can build the excitement with music or drumming. Or you can just have someone lay the broom down in front of you, jump it and continue straight into the recessional without explanation or fanfare.

Because it is made of straw, a broom is linked with wheat, a potent wedding fertility symbol. An old superstition from the British Isles is that, to protect the home against witches, a new bride should place a broom across the threshold together with a bowl of salt. It was believed that witches have to count the straws in the broom and the grains of salt before they can enter the house, and since it would be impossible to complete this task between midnight and dawn, the home and the couple would be protected. So it was customary to give the couple a broom, together with bread, for food, and salt, symbol of faithfulness and purity. The broom was used to symbolically sweep obstacles out of the path of the bride and groom before they entered their home for the first time as a married couple.

Jumping the broom at the conclusion of a marriage ceremony has also been a featured in other cultures for a very long time. It is one of the oldest marriage traditions from the British Isles and Welsh, Scottish, Roma (Gypsy), and Wiccan marriage ceremonies included some form of broom-jumping to symbolize transition into married life, for fertility and to signify their joint acceptance of the ordinary tasks of everyday domestic life.

For African-American couples, the ritual celebrates the spirit of their African heritage. At a time when slaves were forbidden to marry in certain southern states, using a benign domestic object was a relatively safe way to express lifelong commitment because it was unlikely to arouse suspicion in the minds of slave owners. Some slave owners, however, promoted the practice and attended the celebration, as documented in a account of a nineteenth century occurrence collected as part of the 1930 Works Progress Administration slavery oral history project

> *Well, dey just lay de broom down, 'n' dem what's gwine to git marry' walks out 'n' steps ober dat broom bofe togedder, 'n' de old massa, he say, 'I now pronounce you man 'n' wife' 'n' den dey was t'it – con ce-mony, no license, no nothin', jis' marryin'.*

In the years immediately after the abolition of slavery the practice all but disappeared, but Alex Haley's novel *Roots*, and the movie based on the novel, inspired a revival in the latter years of the 20th century.

Most couples decorate the broom in some way, using ribbons and/or flowers. Choosing flowers for their symbolic significance, such as roses for love and ivy for fidelity and friendship, can add to the symbolism.

I like to suggest that the couple joins hands, and then together they jump the broom (both feet in the air), take another step then turn to one another and kiss again before proceeding back up the aisle.

Example Words for your Jumping of the Broom

Your selection from the words below may be mixed, matched, and edited to create a broom jumping ritual that is very personal to you. Where appropriate, substitute *union* or *partnership* for the word *marriage*. Even better, let the examples below inspire you to create your own words for your program or for your celebrant to speak. There is a template in the Appendix.

1. *The celebrant (officiant) asks for the broom to be brought forward. The area in front of the couple is swept as the celebrant (officiant) explains the ritual)*

   The broom, symbol of domesticity, denotes a counter-balance and counter-dependency between Elizabeth and Charles, with both mutually working and sharing responsibilities for the benefit, well-being, and protection of each other and of their immediate and extended families. The broom is also a symbol of change. Jumping the broom represents leaving behind one life while jumping whole-heartedly into another. _____ has symbolically swept any obstacles to their happiness out of _____ and _____'s path.

   _____ *lays the broom down in front of* _____ *and* _____ *who jump the broom, take a step forward together and share a second kiss.*

2. Jumping the broom represents the crossing of the threshold from their single life to life as a couple, and brings good luck. Please welcome _____ and _____ as they leap into married life together.

_____ *lays the broom down in front of* _____ *and* _____ *who jump the broom, take a step forward together and share a second kiss.*

3. _____ and _____ know that they are stronger together than they are alone. They have chosen to take the leap into married life with joy, faith, and a firm commitment that theirs will be a marriage rooted in love.

The celebrant (officiant) asks _____ *to bring the broom forward*

They will make this broom a part of their home, where they will hang it as a symbol of this happy day and the love that binds them together and holds them close. It will also remind them of your love and support.

The broom is laid across the aisle. _____ *and* _____ *join hands*

Please join me in counting to three to encourage _____ and _____ to leap high as they leap over the broom.

Everyone: "One, Two, Three!"

_____ *and* _____ *jump over the broom together and then kiss before continuing down the aisle.*

4. **An explanation suitable for an intercultural ceremony**

_____, it has long been an African-American tradition that the bride and groom jump a broom at the end of their marriage ceremony to symbolize their entrance into domestic bliss. I've asked _____ to place a broom across your path in celebration of this custom.

5. **An explanation suitable for a same-sex couple**:

The celebrant (officiant) asks for the broom to be brought forward. The area in front of the couple is swept as the celebrant (officiant) explains the ritual). In times past in England, Scotland, and Wales couples jumped the broom as a declaration of common-law marriage, a custom of great antiquity dating back to the time of the druids. The broom, symbol of domesticity, symbolizes _____ and _____'s intention to share responsibilities for the benefit, well-being, and protection of one another and of their immediate and extended families. _____ has symbolically swept any obstacles to their happiness out of _____ and _____'s path.

PART SEVEN: RECEPTION DEPARTURES

FAREWELL CIRCLE

A simple, easy to organize and intimate way of concluding your wedding reception, a farewell circle seems to be very Australian way of taking your leave from your guests. Because it is not a custom that is widely practised anywhere else in the world, your guests will see it as something unique and inclusive.

When you are ready to take your leave, your Master of Ceremonies asks your guests to form a large circle round you, and you then move round the circle, personally thanking your guests and bidding them farewell.

However, if you have a larger number of guests, the process can be long and drawn out for those patiently waiting in line. You can halve waiting time by splitting up, and moving round the circle in opposite directions. You can also encourage things to move quickly by having your DJ or band play a lively and recognizable tune such as *Wish me luck as you wave me goodbye*, by not scheduling a farewell circle if you have more than 80-100 guests, or by having a farewell circle of a different sort. Borrow the old Scottish custom, and have everyone join hands in a circle and *Auld Lang Syne*, and then make a quick exit.

FAREWELL ARCH

A farewell arch is an informal, upbeat and fun way for a couple to exit the reception. It takes only a few minutes to set up. Your Master of Ceremonies asks your guests to form up two rows and to join their raised hands with those of the person directly opposite forming a long tunnel-like arch through which you run.

FAREWELL GUARD OF HONOR

A farewell guard of honor is similar to a farewell arch but without people joining hands. This enables you to walk upright and at a more leisurely pace, taking time to informally talk to your guests and to thank them personally for sharing your special day and for their good wishes and gifts.

FIREWORKS

Spectacular fireworks displays are becoming a more and more common addition to weddings. While usually scheduled to signal the end of the reception, fireworks can mark the end of the ceremony if the venue, the time of day and the time of year allows this. Many pyrotechnic companies also offer indoor fireworks, including fountains. Outdoors you can have fountains along your exit path or driveway, or a regular fireworks show for everyone to enjoy.

Decisions you will have to make include:
- When and where the fireworks display will take place
- How long will it last. As you might expect, the longer the display the more expensive it will be. Fireworks displays lose their impact after quite short time. Five minutes of high quality display with a variety of effects and sequences will be more than enough to delight everyone.
- Whether you will accept a standard display or would prefer a customized one, which will cost more.
- Whether you want the display to be set to music. Having a professional fireworks display choreographed to music that has meaning in your relationship can be very special, but will be expensive. To save money use one of the company's standard displays.

- Whether you want to include fire writing (your names and perhaps the date, perhaps on either side of a flaming heart).

A Word of Caution: Always consult with your venue regarding its policy in relation to fireworks, and ensure you understand local noise restrictions. Your chosen pyrotechnics company may be able to use low noise. If you are marrying during the summer . If you are marrying during the summer in an area where there is a risk of a total fire ban being imposed, your fireworks display may have to be cancelled at the last minute.

APPENDIX

WORKSHEET: Our recessional participants
Participants and order of our processional

Who will cue the start of the music?

How?

Who will cue the recessional?

How?

WORKSHEET: Our recessional music

Who will provide the music?

Live   Recorded

☐ Singer accompanied by   ☐ **CD Player**

_____   ☐ **iPod**

☐ Solo Musician

☐ Type of instrument

_____

☐ Duo

☐ Type of instruments

_____

_____

☐ Trio

☐ Type of instruments

_____

_____

☐ Quartet

☐ Type of instruments

_____

_____

☐ Quintent

☐ Type of instruments

_____

_____

☐ Mixed

  ☐ Type _____

Name and contact details of musician(s) or person responsible for operating the recorded music

Music choice for Recessional

WORKSHEET: Our arch of honor

Type

☐ Military _____

☐ Sporting _____

☐ Interest_____

Permissions required

Who will participate and how?

Supplies required

Suppliers

TEMPLATE: Words for our arch of honor

For our program or order of service

WORKSHEET: Our wedding bells

Type

- ☐ Church Bells
- ☐ Mobile Bell Peal
- ☐ Recorded Bells
- ☐ Truce Bell
- ☐ Sound Blessing

Permissions required

Who will participate and how?

Supplies required

Suppliers

TEMPLATE: Words for our wedding bells

For tags or signs (if required)

For our program or order of service

For our Officiant

WORKSHEET: Our recessional toss

Type of Toss

Type of Toss	Container
☐ Bubbles	☐ **Individual**
☐ Petals	☐ Box
☐ Type _____	☐ Calico/Muslin Bag
☐ Herbs	☐ Cellophane Bag
☐ Type _____	☐ Cone
☐ Leaves	☐ Glassine Envelope
☐ Type _____	☐ Organza Bag
☐ Mixed	☐ Other _____
☐ Type _____	_____
	☐ **Fill your own**

Where and when will the toss take place

☐ As we walk down the aisle

☐ After we've exited the church/chapel/ceremony space

☐ Other

Permissions/Notifications required

Who will participate

Supplies required

Suppliers

TEMPLATE: Toss tag words

For signs near the baskets of tosses

For the toss tags

For our program or order of service

.

WORKSHEET: Our wedding release

Ritual or Release

- ☐ Balloon Release
- ☐ Butterfly Release
- ☐ Dove Release
- ☐ Sky Lantern Release

Permissions required

Who will participate in the release and how?

Supplies required

Suppliers

TEMPLATE: Words for our wedding release

For our program or order of service

For our Officiant/Master of Ceremonies

WORKSHEET: Our conclusion ritual

Type of Ritual

- ☐ Breaking the Glass
- ☐ Breaking the Vase
- ☐ Jumping the Broom

Who will participate and how?

Supplies required

Suppliers

TEMPLATE: Words for our conclusion ritual

For our program

For our Master of Ceremonies

WORKSHEET: Our reception departure

Type

- ☐ Farewell Circle
- ☐ Farewell Arch
- ☐ Guard of Honor
- ☐ Fireworks

Permissions required

Who will participate and how?

Music choice

Played by

Supplies required

Suppliers

TEMPLATE: Words for our reception departure

For our program

For our officiant/Master of Ceremonies

ABOUT THE AUTHOR

J ennifer Cram is a professional marriage celebrant (wedding officiant) appointed by the Attorney General to officiate marriages in all states and territories of Australia. She is currently based in Brisbane, Queensland, where each year she creates and officiates more than a hundred marriage ceremonies. She also officiates numerous commitment ceremonies for same sex couples.

Born in Australia and raised in Africa, Jennifer (or Jenny as she is known to her family, her friends, and the couples she works with) comes from a family that for five generations has moved between Australia, Africa and the United States. One of her great-great-grandfathers was a forty-niner, her great-grandfather and her great-uncle worked on the reconstruction of San Francisco after the 1906 earthquake, and she herself lived for some time in New York City as a young woman. A skilled and experienced writer, public speaker, and choreographer, Jennifer has numerous academic qualifications in Celebrancy and holds degrees in Literature, Psychology, Information Science, and Management. She brings all those skills to the development and performance of ceremonies, together her knowledge and experience of multiple cultures and sensitivity to cultural nuances.

Appreciated by wedding photographers for her attention to the visual aspects of the ceremony and for the way she ensures photogenic moments of warm and natural interaction between the couple and between the couple, their bridal party, and the guests, she has devoted a great deal of time to researching and developing a wide range of alternative ways to include and personalize rituals in ceremonies. In 2013 she was voted the best marriage celebrant in her state in the Australian Bridal Industry Awards. In 2010, 2011, an 2013 she was also rated one of the top 0.1% of Australian marriage celebrants.

To learn more about Jennifer or enquire about booking her for a ceremony go to www.jennifercram.com.au or read on for some comments from photographers and couples:

Our favorite part of the wedding was seeing people so engaged in what was happening. The best thing about the ceremony was the tone set by you, Jenny. it made everyone relax and feel part of what was happening. **- Holly and Neil**

We felt special and we are still talking of how our wedding ceremony was beautiful. Thank You Jenny it was fantastic, you were amazing you left everyone including our families who had celebrants for their wedding amazed at how ours was special, "People were talking" high recommendations!!! My sister-in-law who is next in line to be married has clearly specified she would be having you conduct her wedding. Our guests felt that you were different from other celebrants. We look forward to renewing our vows with you. No wonder you are No 1 Celebrant in QLD. **- Penny & Grant**

Choosing Jenny as our celebrant was one of the best decisions we made for our wedding. Our ceremony was perfect, everything we imagined and more. It was so "us". We have already recommended Jenny to friends. Thank you for making our day so amazing. You made everyone feel included amd went above and beyond in your duties. There was no stress at all **- Amber and Anthony**

You did a fantastic job of arranging what we had said in our survey and presenting it in a way that our guests felt they knew us even better. It was so personal and joyful, but also relaxed and entertaining like we asked for. We were *both thrilled and over-the-moon happy. The way your performed the ceremony was beautifully done and appreciated by all. I personally am very grateful for your assistance fleshing out my vows. You, again, were great with all of this. You were fantastic with paperwork and legal requirements and we truly appreciate all of your help. -***Adam & Kimberly. Kimberly's mother commented on Facebook:** *Jennifer, thank you so much for the beautiful, personal, poignant ceremony you performed for Kimberly and Adam yesterday. From America, a civil celebrant ceremony was new to me and it really touched my heart. Thank you for all you did!*

Everyone mentioned how they loved the ceremony, and were very glad they were able to join in and have a laugh. It fit our family perfectly, and I am so glad it turned out perfectly. We passed on your business card to our friends, a young couple there, as they enjoyed the service very much. Everyone was thrilled by both the LGBT statement (which made a few people in the audience come up to me and thank me profusely for including it). **- Anne and Jack**

Thank you so so much for Saturday. The ceremony was wonderful. Many people have said it was the best wedding ceremony they have ever been to. I know people say that all the time but I actually believe them. It was wonderful, thoughtful and personal and my family and friends have said they loved your delivery and dry sense of humour along with the personal touches. We are so delighted that we chose you as our celebrant and would certainly have no hesitation in recommending you in the future. Bye for now but hopefully our paths will cross again. **Katie and Lachie**

We asked Jenny for a simple ceremony that was no fuss yet still memorable to us and she delivered. We are so grateful that she took care in what we wanted but still added a little touch of her own magic to make our day one that we would never forget. Thank you for a beautiful day! We enjoyed every moment. Jenny created a ceremony that was unique for us and we didn't feel pressured into doing anything we didn't want to do. it was good that we could have a laugh as well, that was very important to us. - **Terese and Dion**

Jenny I have had the pleasure of working with you many times and I can honestly say that every time has been beautiful, intimate and personal. Experience counts for a lot, but it isn't just experience or the age of a person that makes a ceremony for a couple, it is a person who has a beautiful soul and puts that into their work that truly makes it a unforgettable and personal experience for the couples. The genuine emotions that you bring out in couples are such beautiful moments for them to share and from a photographers standpoint make our job even more special to be able to be part of and document for our couples. - **Scott Lawler of Scott Lawler Photography**

At least two dozen people commented to us that our ceremony was the best they had ever seen and we are still receiving texts with similar comments today. We just can't thank you enough for creating a fabulous ceremony that was so warm, fun and very personal. - **Email from Liz and Cameron the day after their wedding at the Glen Hotel.**

Jennifer Cram is a shining example of excellence in her profession. Her ability to listen, ask the right questions and gently guide us produced the perfect ceremony. Every part of the ceremony was infused with Darren and my personalities. We have received countless comments from guests about our ceremony and their impression of Jenny, all glowing and very touching. I even had one friend say she was 'hanging on Jenny's every word. Jenny Cram helped make such perfect memories for all at our wedding. We are deeply indebted. -**Jannine and Darren**

From our very first phone call to Jennifer we found her approach to be comfortable, calm and competent, whilst being professional yet personal. These thoughts were proved during our first face-to-face meeting. Communication frequency was appropriate. We had given Jennifer specific ideas and expectations of her as a Celebrant and at no time were we disappointed with her suggestions and ideas and final product. Jennifer conducted the ceremony in such manner allowing our love to shine. Barely a dry eye in the house our guests commented it was the best, most meaningful, personalised civil ceremony they have ever attended. We would have absolutely no hesitation in recommending Jennifer. We provide this testimonial with our heartfelt thanks. Kind regards and love - **Craig & James**